THE SWEATER CONNECTION

OVER 25 DESIGNS TO KNIT FOR PRETEENS AND TEENS

MICHELE MAKS

BALLANTINE BOOKS   NEW YORK

Library of Congress Catalog Card Number: 87-91354

ISBN: 0-345-33278-4

Text design by Michaelis/Carpelis Design Associates

Photography by Steve Moore

Styling by Barbara Aria

Illustrations by Patrick O'Brien

Cover design by Richard Aquan

Manufactured in the United States of America

First Edition: January 1989

10 9 8 7 6 5 4 3 2 1

THE SWEATER CONNECTION

WITHDRAWN

TO PAT HARSTE, WHO OPENED THE DOOR

ACKNOWLEDGMENTS

Without the help of several knitters, I never would have finished this book. I would like to thank Sue Buck, Lois King, Nancy LaPlante, and Jack Carson for their dedication to the cause. I must also thank Jack and Quayl for doing much of the "dog work"—sewing on buttons, tying up loose ends, deciphering my charts, and so on. Thanks also to the many yarn companies who contributed to the book, as well as to Michelle Russell and Karen Hwa of Ballantine for believing in the concept and putting up with a very temperamental (i.e., *grouchy*) designer.

Contents

THE SWEATER CONNECTION

I began to knit at the age of ten, when I was introduced to the craft through a summer recreation program. One of my earliest thrills was going into Woolworth's to buy one skein of every single variegated yarn they carried. Ecstasy! I was hooked for life. My taste in yarns has changed somewhat over the years, but my passion for yarns and fiber has only increased.

As a teenager, knitting for myself was very frustrating, and it's a wonder that I didn't give it up. There were many patterns available, but nothing *I* would wear. Fortunately, my sister had three kids, so at least I could always make mittens for them. Also, I had an extremely vague notion about what "gauge" actually meant—quite frequently, there were items to unmake as well.

Eventually I found help. When I had trouble with a knitting project I could bring it to a boy friend (not a *boyfriend*), who had learned the finer points of the craft from his sister. In exchange for his assistance, I taught him how to throw a javelin, a skill I had learned from my brother. (Knitting was the one and only "feminine" thing I did as an adolescent.) My friend's help was invaluable because, up until then, if I made an error I had to rip out the whole sweater. I just couldn't figure out how to unravel a few inches and get the stitches back on the needles. This is an illustration not of how stupid I am but that one *can* persevere and get it right.

Living on Long Island, in close proximity to both New York City and the Hamptons, gave me an awareness of fashion. When I later moved to a farm in Maine and took charge of six children (four of my own and two stepchildren), a different reality was added to my sense of style. Long, cold winters and the mud season made warmth and practicality a major concern. The kids needed, and got, a bunch of really great sweaters.

But I learned that knitting for teenagers can be a real pain. Their idea of fashion has an elusive quality to it that bears no arguments. A sweater either makes it or lies in the closet (usually on the floor in the back). Contrary to popular opinion, boys are no easier to please than girls, *and* there are fewer patterns for them. My design work for magazines, as well as my own "in-house" experiences, showed me the enormous need for older children/teens *wearable* knitwear. I hope that the designs in *The Sweater Connection* begin to fill that need.

All of the garments here have met with approval from at least half a dozen not very tactful critics, both male and female, all under the age of sixteen. Many are easy enough for the beginning knitter, and I certainly hope there will be a large number of first attempts as a result. There is nothing as satisfying as completing your first handmade sweater!

MICHELE MAKS

Dear Run Farm

GAUGE

There is something about reading the phrase "To save time, take time to check gauge" in a pattern that inspires me to do otherwise. I am very fortunate in having a consistent, standard gauge in my own handiwork, so I can usually use the recommended yarn and needles and have a garment that matches the pattern's specifications. When the garment hasn't worked out right, I've given it to my husband or one of the kids. Since most people don't have as many children as I do, or husbands who will wear pink sweaters, I recommend working a gauge swatch as a time-saving alternative to making sweaters that don't fit. Needless to say, I myself have given up the practice of ignoring gauge.

The purpose of making a gauge swatch is to find out how many stitches per inch you are knitting up with the yarn used for your project. Knitters differ in how tightly or loosely they work their stitches, so the needle size given in a project's directions is only a suggested size. If your gauge is different from the one stated in the pattern using the recommended needles, you must change the size of the needles.

My standard method of making a gauge swatch is to cast on twenty stitches to the needles suggested. I work a four-inch swatch in the pattern stitch given (often stockinette stitch but not always—be sure to check!). Then I lightly steam press (unless the yarn label warns against doing so), taking care not to stretch the swatch out of shape. Lay the swatch on a hard, flat surface to measure it. Divide twenty by the number of inches (be as exact as possible with your measuring) and you will have the number of stitches per inch, or your gauge. If the number of stitches per inch is smaller than the pattern's gauge, you will need larger needles. If the number of stitches per inch is greater than the pattern's gauge, you will need smaller needles.

The row gauge is figured similarly. Count the number of rows that you have, divide by four (or whatever length in inches you have made your swatch) and you will have the number of rows per inch. In general, the row gauge does not matter as much as the stitch gauge, because most patterns are written to measure by the inch and not the row. The exceptions to this are garments with raglan shaping. If your row gauge is off but your stitch gauge is correct, I would suggest either adding or subtracting rows at the armhole to make up the row gauge difference.

Half a stitch per inch may seem like a small thing to quibble about, but in a complete garment the difference adds up. Let's pretend that you are making a sweater that should measure forty inches around. The back is twenty inches across. The required gauge is four stitches per inch. The directions say to cast on eighty stitches. After working for six inches, you notice that it looks a little small. Measuring confirms your suspicion—it measures seventeen and a half inches across. That means your finished garment will be only thirty-five inches around. You now have the choice of ripping it out or giving it to someone five inches thinner than you had intended. If you had done a gauge swatch, you would have known to use a larger needle than suggested.

A word to the wise about gauge on circular needles: Working a gauge swatch back and forth on a straight needle the same size as your circular needle, or even a small swatch back and forth on that circular needle itself, may mislead you into thinking you are working the proper gauge. My experience (and several of my knitters say the same thing) is that I need a needle one size larger to get the proper gauge in circular knitting than I would if I were working back and forth. This is something that can only be measured by the individual knitter. Regrettably, the only way to check the gauge when knitting in the round is to knit around and around and measure the piece when it's practically too long to tear out comfortably.

One last word of warning: Your state of mind can also affect your gauge, especially in crochet. Beware of picking up your needles after a fight with your better half—you will only produce a too-tight sweater.

SOME BASIC STITCHES

Garter Stitch

Garter Stitch—The simplest of all stitches—merely knit every row.

Reverse Stockinette Stitch

Reverse Stockinette Stitch—Purl all right side rows and knit all wrong side rows. When knitting on circular needles, purl all rows.

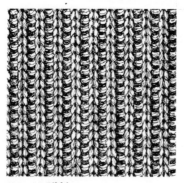
K 1, p 1 Ribbing

Ribbing—In ribbing, there are stitch changes within each row. There are an endless variety of ribbings, but the most common, and the one most used in this book, is a simple k 1 , p 1 rib. For the first row of this rib, knit one stitch, then purl one stitch, and repeat this sequence across the row. With an even number of stitches, you will end with a purl stitch. With an uneven number of stitches, you will end with a knit stitch. To continue in ribbing, you will always knit the knit stitches in the side facing you (they will have a smooth st st look) and purl the purl stitches (they have a ridge).

Stockinette Stitch

Stockinette Stitch—Knit right side rows and purl wrong side rows. When working circularly, knit every round.

WORKING WITH TWO COLORS

There are several different ways to work with more than one color:

Horizontal Stripes—Stripes are the easiest way to use two colors. The new color is joined at the edge of the garment. The loose ends of the old and new yarns are later woven into the seam to finish it off.

Chain Stripe—A single vertical stripe of color worked on top of stitches with a crochet hook. Hold yarn on wrong side of work and draw a loop up with the crochet hook to the right side. Skip two rows, pull up another loop from back of work and slip it through the previous loop. Continue in this manner until desired length of stripe has been worked.

Allover Patterns—Color patterns that are repeated entirely across a row require stranding the yarn across the back of the work. Following your color pattern or chart, work the proper number of stitches

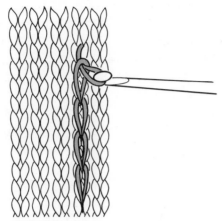

Chain Stripe

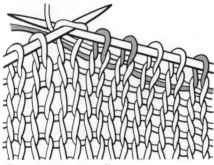

Allover Patterns (stranding yarn)

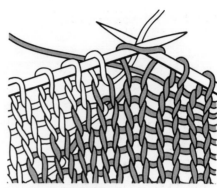

Intarsia (crossing yarns)

comfortably across the work (as in the Snowflake Ragg Pullover). In both of these cases, bobbins or small separate balls of yarn are necessary to work each block of color.

Follow the color chart as in the allover pattern, but cross the yarn and then drop it, using a separate ball of color for each color change. You must cross the yarn at each change or a hole will result.

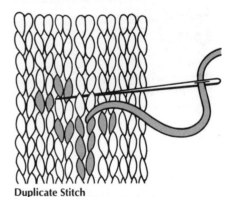

Duplicate Stitch

with the first yarn. Then drop this yarn while twisting with the new one, and work the proper number of stitches with the new yarn. Drop that and twist with the next yarn. It's important to change the direction of the twist from time to time, otherwise you will end up with a horrendous mess of twisted yarn. It's also important not to work too tightly—yarn stranded too tightly will create a gathered effect on the right side of the garment.

It's necessary to recheck your gauge when you've begun an allover color pattern after working with just one color. Many knitters either loosen or tighten up when working with two colors, but simply changing your needle size will solve this problem.

Beginners are advised to stay away from patterns that carry more than two colors per row, at least until they master using just two.

Intarsia—Many patterns call for blocks of color that are not worked across the entire garment. Sometimes a repeated motif is too many stitches away from the previous motif for the yarn to be carried

Duplicate Stitch—This is the practical, lazy man's approach to color patterns that do not involve large blocks of color. Sometimes it is much more relaxing to work a sweater in plain stockinette stitch with one color and worry about embroidering the pattern on later. To work duplicate stitches, use a tapestry needle threaded with yarn. Insert the needle through the center of the stitch from the wrong side to the right side and draw through. Insert the needle from right to left through the top of the stitch, draw yarn through, and insert needle through the center of the same stitch again. You have now covered the original stitch. Continue in this manner for every stitch in your color pattern.

BLOCKING

Before sewing up the separate pieces of your fresh-ly knitted garment, each piece should be blocked. Quite frequently, the yarn wrapper will have special instructions concerning blocking. For instance, some acrylic yarns will say that blocking is not nec-essary, while garments of most other fibers will look and wear more attractively if blocked.

Blocking is not a mysterious process. A flat, hard surface covered with a heavy blanket, an iron, and a damp towel to place on top of the garment are really all you need. Lay the garment pieces out flat and pin to the blanket in the specifications given in the pat-tern. It is important when pinning the pieces not to twist the fabric and to keep all the rows straight. It's also important to use rustless pins.

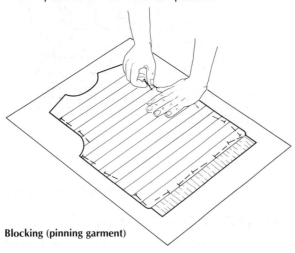

Blocking (pinning garment)

When the pieces are completely laid out, you are ready to block. *Do not press a garment if the yarn label reads ''do not press.''* Some fibers will indeed melt when heat is applied. If there is no such warn-ing, lay the damp towel over the pieces. Place the iron (adjusted to the proper fiber setting) on the tow-el and pick it up. Don't iron back and forth the way you would a shirt—that would distort the knitted gar-ment underneath. Just press the iron down and lift. When this is done over the entire garment, remove the top towel and let the garment dry before remov-ing the pins.

I recommend that you omit the ribbings from the blocking process, pinning only the areas between

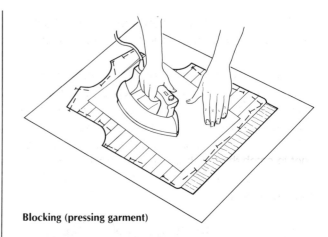

Blocking (pressing garment)

the ribbings and avoiding them while you press. If you wish to press the entire garment, the pins holding the ribbing should be removed during the drying process.

SEAMS

The Knitted Seam Method—Many of the shoulder seams in this book are joined by the knitted seam method. When a shoulder is shaped flat it is very easy to slip the stitches to a holder and join them in this fashion.

Slip the front and back shoulder stitches from the holders onto two needles that are the same size that you used to knit the pieces. Holding the pieces with right sides facing, use a long strand of yarn and a third needle, knit two stitches together twice, each time using one stitch from the front needle and one stitch from the back needle. Bind off one stitch. Con-tinue in this manner until the entire seam is joined. Cut yarn and pull end through the last stitch.

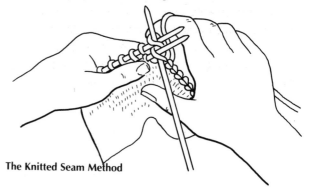

The Knitted Seam Method

If you choose not to use this method, the shoulder stitches may be bound off and later sewn together instead of joined.

The Backstitch Seam—For a backstitch seam, place the right sides of the garment together. Matching the patterns on each side, take a long strand of yarn and backstitch into the center of each stitch about one-quarter inch from the edge, taking care not to catch the top, bound-off, stitches in the seam. You can use the backstitch seam method on side seams as well.

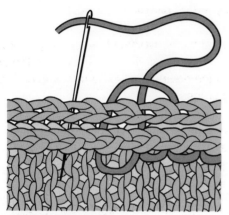

The Backstitch Seam

The Edge-to-Edge Seam—This is another method that is especially suited to stockinette stitch garments. This seam is practically invisible and doesn't form a lump on the side of the garment the way a backstitched seam can.

Place the two pieces of the garment together side by side, edges touching, matching the pattern or stitches row by row. With the main color, sew into the top of each stitch alternately.

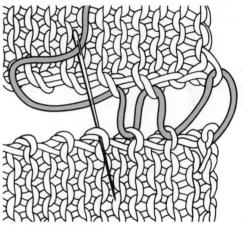

The Edge-to-Edge Seam

MAKING YARN SUBSTITUTIONS

A list of the yarns, and the companies who supplied them, used for the photographed garments appears in the back of the book. Since there is a great deal of turnover in specific lines of yarn from year to year, you may have to make substitutions if the original yarn is not available. Your yarn store can be very helpful in finding a substitute when necessary or desired. Whenever you substitute a yarn, though, and indeed before you begin *any* project, take the time to work up a gauge swatch. It is absolutely essential for checking not only the number of stitches and rows but the feel of the knitted fabric as well. The proper number of stitches per inch won't matter if your fabric feels like a piece of iron or droops like a dishrag when worked up.

ABBREVIATIONS

Learning to knit or crochet involves learning a new language of abbreviations and symbols. It is easier to read a pattern if you take the time to learn some of these abbreviations before starting.

beg	beginning
CC	contrasting color
ch	chain
cm	centimeter(s)
dc	double crochet
dec	decrease
dp	double-pointed
inc	increase
k	knit
MC	main color
mm	millimeter(s)
oz	ounce(s)
p	purl
psso	pass slip stitch over
rem	remaining
rnd(s)	round(s)
sc	single crochet
sl	slip
sl st	slip stitch
st(s)	stitch(es)
st st	stockinette stitch
tog	together
tr	treble crochet
yd	yard(s)
yo	yarn over

THE SWEATER CONNECTION

CAMOUFLAGE-AND-SUEDE PULLOVER

**BOYS LOVE CAMOUFLAGE WEAR! THIS SWEATER IS MADE
EXTRA SPECIAL WITH THE ADDITION OF SUEDE PATCHES AT THE ELBOWS AND SHOULDERS.**

SIZES:
Directions are for boy's small, with medium and large in parentheses. Finished chest measurements 36 (39⅓,42)"/91.5 (99,106.5) cm; length to back neck edge 23 (25,27)"/57.5 (62.5,67.5) cm; armhole measures 16 (18,20)"/40.5 (45.5,51) cm; length of sleeve from underarm 18 (19,20)"/45.5 (48,51) cm.

MATERIALS:
10½ (12¼,14) oz/300 (350,400) gr sport yarn in spinach (MC), 5¼ (7,7) oz/150 (200,200) gr moss green (CC), and 1¾ (3½,3½) oz/30 (100,100) gr tartan green (A) and saddle brown (B)
2 pairs brown suede elbow patches (for shoulders and elbows)

NEEDLES:
One pair each size 4/3.5mm and 6/4mm knitting needles, or size needed to obtain gauge
6 stitch holders
yarn needle

GAUGE:
11 sts = 2"/5cm and 7 rows = 1"/2.5cm on size 6 needles over st st

BACK:
With smaller needles and MC, cast on 100 (108,116) sts. Work in k 2, p 2 rib for 2"/5cm. Change to larger needles. Work in st st until 14 (15,16) "/35.5 (38,40.5) cm from beg. End with right side facing.

SHAPE ARMHOLES:
Bind off 6 sts at beg of next 2 rows. Work even in st st until armhole measures 8 (9,10) "/20 (23,25.5) cm. Sl 28 (31,34) sts on holder for right shoulder, sl next 32 (34,36) sts to holder for neckband, sl rem 28 (31,34) sts to holder for left shoulder.

FRONT:
Work same as for back until armhole measures 6 (7,8) "/15 (18,20) cm. End with right side facing.

SHAPE NECK:
K 32 (35,38) sts; turn. Sl next 24 (26,28) sts to holder for neck. With new strand of MC, work to end. Working both sides simultaneously, dec 1 st at each neck edge on next k row, then every other row 3 times more. Work even until same length as back to shoulder. Sl sts to holders for shoulder seams.

SLEEVES:
With smaller needles and CC, cast on 48 (52,52) sts. Work in k 2, p 2 ribbing for 2½"/6cm. Change to larger needles and st st. Inc 1 st on next row, then every 4th row until there are 88 (100,110) sts. Work even until sleeve measures 18 (19,20) "/45.5 (48,51) cm. Bind off.

NECKBAND:

Join right shoulder seam. With smaller needles and MC, k and p into each st of back neck holder, pick up and k 18 sts to front neck holder, k across front neck holder, pick up 18 sts to shoulder edge, 124 (130,136) sts. Work in k 1, p 1 ribbing for 3/4"/2cm. Bind off loosely in ribbing.

FINISHING:

Working in duplicate stitch, follow charts for camouflage pattern, taking care to keep work flat. Steam lightly, omitting ribbings. Weave left shoulder seam including neckband. Center sleeves on shoulder seam and sew in place. Sew side and sleeve seams. Sew one pair of elbow patches on shoulders and the other on elbows.

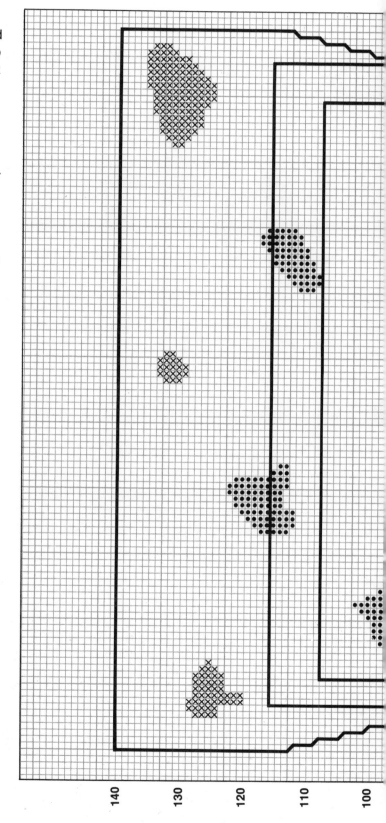

KEY:

⬤ = A (tartan green)

☒ = B (saddle brown)

140 130 120 110 100

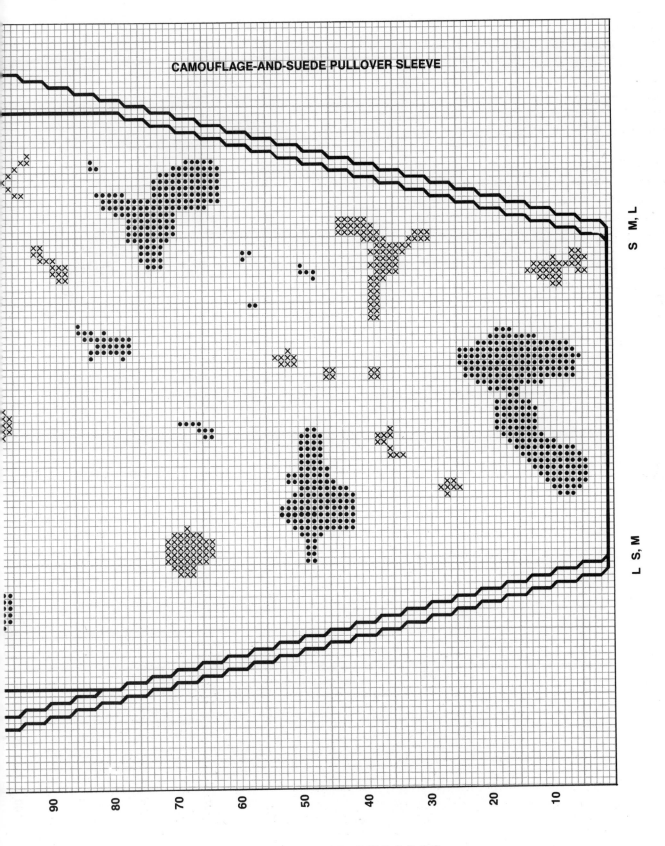

CAMOUFLAGE-AND-SUEDE PULLOVER SLEEVE

S M, L

L S, M

90   80   70   60   50   40   30   20   10

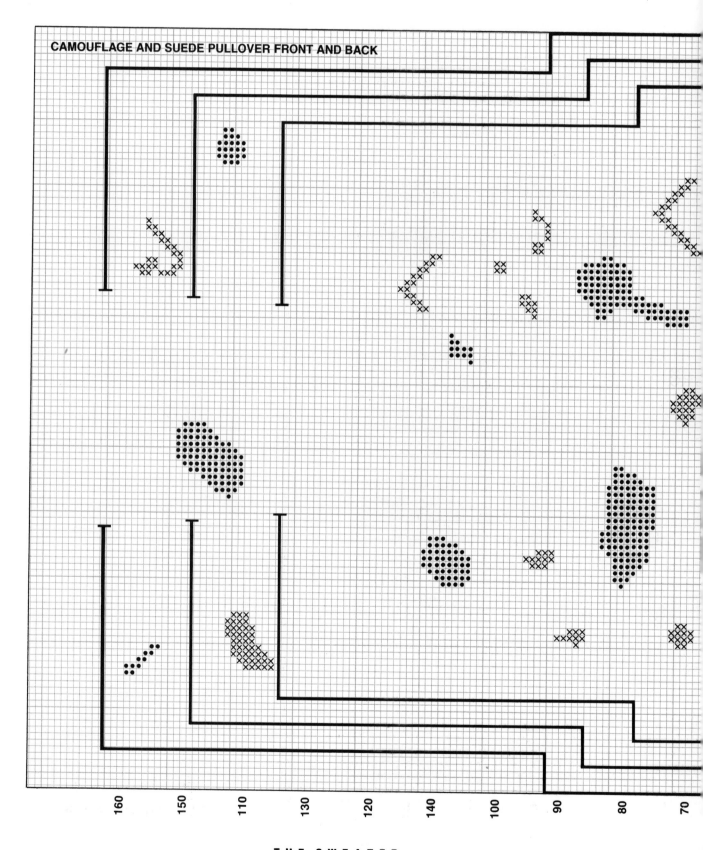

CAMOUFLAGE AND SUEDE PULLOVER FRONT AND BACK

160   150   110   130   120   140   100   90   80   70

KEY:

● = A (tartan green)

✕ = B (saddle brown)

PEPLUMED DIAMONDS

RUFFLES AT THE NECK AND SLEEVES TEAMED WITH A SOFT-COLORED, FLUFFY YARN MAKE THIS A VERY FEMININE SWEATER. A PEPLUM ADDS JUST THE RIGHT VICTORIAN TOUCH.

SIZES
Directions are for girl's small, with medium and large in parentheses. Finished chest measurements 34½ (36½,39½)"/87 (92,100) cm; length from waist to back neck edge 18½ (19½,21)"/46 (49,53.5) cm; armhole measures 12¾ (13½,14¼)"/32.5 (34,36) cm; length of sleeve at underarm (including cuff) 16½ (17½,18½)"/42 (45,47) cm.

MATERIALS
12¼ (14,15¾) oz/350 (400,450) gr worsted weight brushed acrylic yarn

NEEDLES
One pair each size 5/3.75mm and size 8/5mm needles, or size needed to obtain gauge
2 stitch holders

GAUGE
4 sts and 6 rows = 1"/2.5cm on size 8 needles in pattern stitch; 4 sts and 5 rows = 1"/2.5cm on size 8 needles over st st

BACK
With smaller needles and MC, cast on 69 (73,79) sts. K for 4 rows. Change to larger needles and work in pattern as follows:
Row 1: K 9 (6,9), p 1, *k 9, p 1; repeat from * across; end k 9 (6,9).
Row 2 and all even-numbered rows: K the k sts and p the p sts as they face you.
Row 3: K 8 (5,8), *p 1, k 1, p 1, k 7; repeat from * across; end p 1, k 1, p 1, k 8 (5,8).
Row 5: K 7 (4,7), *p 1, k 3, p 1, k 5; repeat from * across; end p 1, k 3, p 1, k 7 (4,7).
Row 7: K 6 (3,6), *p 1, k 5, p 1, k 3; repeat from * across; end p 1, k 5, p 1, k 6 (3,6).
Row 9: K 5 (2,5), *p 1, k 7, p 1, k 1; repeat from * across; end p 1, k 7, p 1, k 5 (2,5).
Row 11: K 4 (1,4), *p 1, k 9; repeat from * across; end p 1, k 4, (1,4).
Row 13: Repeat row 9.
Row 15: Repeat row 7.
Row 17: Repeat row 5.
Row 19: Repeat row 3.
Row 20: Repeat row 2.

Work rows 1 to 10 once more. Change to smaller needles and work in k 1, p 1 ribbing for 2"/5cm. Continue in pattern, beg row 11, until 11½ (12,13)"/28.5 (30.5,33) cm from ribbing. End with right side facing.

SHAPE ARMHOLES
Keeping to pattern, bind off 4 sts at beg of next 2 rows, then 1 st each edge every other row 4 times. Continue in pattern until armhole measures 7 (7½,8)"/18 (19,20) cm. End with right side facing.

SHAPE SHOULDERS
Bind off 6 (6,7) sts at beg of next 4 rows, then 6 (7,7) sts at beg of next 2 rows. Sl rem 17 (19,21) sts to holder for neckband.

FRONT
Work as for back until armhole measures 5 (5½,6)"/12.5 (14,15) cm. End with right side facing.

SHAPE NECK
Mark center 11 (13,15) sts. Keeping to pattern, work to first marker, with second strand, work to the next marker, sl sts between markers to holder for neckband, work to end. Working both sides simultaneously, dec 1 st each neck edge every other row 3 times. Work even until same length as back to shoulders. Bind off for shoulders from each outside edge as for back.

SLEEVES
With larger needles and MC, cast on 51 (54,57) sts. K 4 rows. Continue in st st until 1½"/4 cm from beg. End right side facing. Dec as follows: *k 1, k 2 tog; repeat from * across, end last repeat k 1 (0,1), 34 (36,38) sts. Change to smaller needles and continue in k 1, p 1 ribbing for 2¼"/6cm. Change to larger needles and inc as follows: * k 1, k 2 into next st; repeat from *, 51 (54,57) sts. Work even in st st until 15 (16,17)"/38 (40.5,43) cm from beg of ribbing. End with right side facing.

CAP SHAPING
Bind off 4 sts at beg of next 2 rows, then dec 1 st each edge every other row 4 times. Work even until 4¾ (5,5⅓)"/12 (12.5,13) cm from beg of cap shaping. End with right side facing. K 2 tog across; end k 1 (0,1). Bind off all sts.

FINISHING
Block pieces lightly. Sew left shoulder seam. Neckband: With smaller needles, inc 1 st in each st across back neck holder, pick up and k 20 sts to front neck holder, k across sts from front neck holder, pick up and k 20 sts to shoulder. Work in k 1, p 1 ribbing for 1"/2.5cm. Change to larger needles and st st (k on right side of collar, p wrong side of sweater), and inc as follows: *k 1, inc 1 st in next st; repeat from * across. Work 5 more rows st st. K 3 rows. Bind off loosely in k. Sew right shoulder seam including neckband. Sew in sleeves. Sew side and sleeve seams.

GLITTERY DIAMONDS

THE SAME DIAMOND PATTERN FROM PEPLUMED DIAMONDS TAKES ON A MODERN LOOK WHEN KNIT IN A GLITTERY YARN WITHOUT THE RUFFLES.

SIZES

Directions are for girl's small, with medium and large in parentheses. Finished chest measurements 34½ (36½,39½)"/87 (92,100) cm; length to back neck edge 18½ (19½,21)"/46 (49,53.5) cm; armhole measures 12¾ (13½,14¼)"/32.5 (34,36) cm; length of sleeve from underarm 15 (16,17)"/38 (40.5,43) cm.

MATERIALS

10½ (12¼,14) oz/300 (350,400) gr worsted weight brushed acrylic yarn.

NEEDLES

One pair each size 6/4mm and size 8/5mm, or size needed to obtain gauge
2 stitch holders

GAUGE

4 sts and 6 rows = 1"/2.5cm on size 8 needles in pattern st; 4 sts and 5 rows = 1"/2.5cm on size 8 needles over st st

BACK

With smaller needles and MC, cast on 69 (73,79) sts. Work in k 1, p 1 ribbing for 2"/5cm. Change to larger needles and work in pattern as follows:
Row 1: K 9 (6,9), p 1, *k 9, p 1; repeat from * across; end k 9 (6,9).

Row 2 and all even-numbered rows: K the k sts and p the p sts as they face you.
Row 3: K 8 (5,8), *p 1, k 1, p 1, k 7; repeat from * across; end p 1, k 1, p 1, k 8 (5,8).
Row 5: K 7 (4,7), *p 1, k 3, p 1, k 5; repeat from * across; end p 1, k 3, p 1, k 7 (4,7).
Row 7: K 6 (3,6), *p 1, k 5, p 1, k 3; repeat from * across; end p 1, k 5, p 1, k 6 (3,6).

Row 9: K 5 (2,5), *p 1, k 7, p 1, k 1; repeat from * across; end p 1, k 7, p 1, k 5 (2,5).
Row 11: K 4 (1,4), *p 1, k 9; repeat from * across; end p 1, k 4, (1,4).

Row 13: Repeat row 9.
Row 15: Repeat row 7.
Row 17: Repeat row 5.
Row 19: Repeat row 3.
Row 20: Repeat row 2.
Work even in pattern, repeating these 20 rows, until 11½ (12,13)"/28.5 (30.5,33) cm from beg. End with right side facing.

SHAPE ARMHOLES
Keeping to pattern, bind off 4 sts at beg of next 2 rows, then 1 st each edge every other row 4 times. Continue in pattern until armhole measures 7 (7½,8)"/18 (19,20) cm. End with right side facing.

SHAPE SHOULDERS
Bind off 6 (6,7) sts at beg of next 4 rows, then 6 (7,7) sts at beg of next 2 rows. Sl rem 17 (19,21) sts to holder for neckband.

FRONT
Work as for back until armhole measures 5 (5½,6)"/12.5 (14,15) cm. End with right side facing.

SHAPE NECK
Mark center 11 (13,15) sts. Keeping to pattern, work to first marker, with second strand, work to next marker, sl sts between markers to holder for neckband, work to end. Working both sides simulta-

neously, dec 1 st each neck edge every other row 3 times. Work even until same length as back to shoulders. Bind off for shoulders from each outside edge as for back.

SLEEVES
With smaller needles, cast on 33 (35,37) sts. Work in k 1, p 1 ribbing for 2¼"/6cm; inc 1 st at end of last row. Change to larger needles and inc as follows: K 1, *inc in next st, k 1; repeat from * across, 51 (54,57) sts. Work even in st st until 15 (16,17)"/38 (40.5,43) cm from beg. End with right side facing.

CAP SHAPING
Bind off 4 sts at beg of next 2 rows, then dec 1 st each edge every other row 4 times. Work even until 4¾ (5,5⅓)"/12 (12.5,13) cm from beg of cap shaping. End with right side facing. K 2 tog across; end k 1 (0,1). Bind off all sts.

FINISHING
Block pieces lightly. Sew left shoulder seam. Neckband: With smaller needles and MC, inc 1 st in each st across back neck holder, pick up and k 20 sts to front neck holder, k across sts from front neck holder, pick up and k 20 sts to shoulder. Work in k 1, p 1 ribbing for 1"/2.5cm. Bind off loosely in ribbing. Sew right shoulder and neckband seams. Sew in sleeves. Sew side and sleeve seams.

ARROW RAGLAN

THIS PULLOVER SAYS "LOOK AT ME!" A FUN-TO-WEAR ALTERNATIVE TO THAT OLD SWEATSHIRT.

SIZES
Directions are for boy's small, with medium and large in parentheses. Finished chest measurements 36 (38,41)"/91.5 (96.5,104) cm; armhole measures 15 (17,19½)"/38 (43,49.5) cm; length of sleeve from underarm 16 (17,18)"/40.5 (43,45.5) cm.

MATERIALS
14 (14,17½) oz/400 (400,500) gr knitting worsted in blue (MC), 3½oz/100gr each scarlet (A) and white (B)

NEEDLES
One pair each size 6/4mm and size 8/5mm or size needed to obtain gauge
4 stitch holders
3 bobbins (optional)

GAUGE
4 sts and 6 rows = 1"/2.5cm on size 8 needles over st st

BACK
With smaller needles and A, cast on 73 (77,83) sts. Work in k 1, p 1 ribbing for 2"/5cm. Change to larger needles and MC. Work even in st st until 12 (13,14)"/30.5 (33,35.5) cm from beg. End with right side facing.

SHAPE ARMHOLES
Bind off 3 (2,4) sts at beg of next 2 rows, then dec 1 st each edge every other row 20 (23,24) times. Sl rem 27 sts to holder for neckband.

FRONT
Note: When changing colors, be sure to pick up new color under color just worked to avoid holes. If desired, wind 2 bobbins with MC and 1 bobbin with B.

Cast on and work ribbing as for back. Fasten off. Change to larger needles. With MC, k 26 (28,31); with B, k 21; with MC, k to end. Keeping to color pattern as established, work even until 11 (12,13)"/28 (30.5,33) cm from beg. End with right side facing. Set Arrowhead chart row 1: K 18 (20,23) MC, k 37 B from chart, k 18 (20,23) MC. Continue in st st, following chart and shaping as for back, until 43 sts rem. End with right side facing.

NECK SHAPING
Mark center 21 sts. Continuing raglan dec, work to marker; with 2nd strand of yarn, k to next marker, sl sts between markers to holder, work to end. Working both sides simultaneously, dec 1 st each neck edge every other row 3 times. Work neck edge even while continuing raglan dec until 2 sts rem. K 2 tog.

KEY:

☐ = MC (blue)

⊙ = B (white)

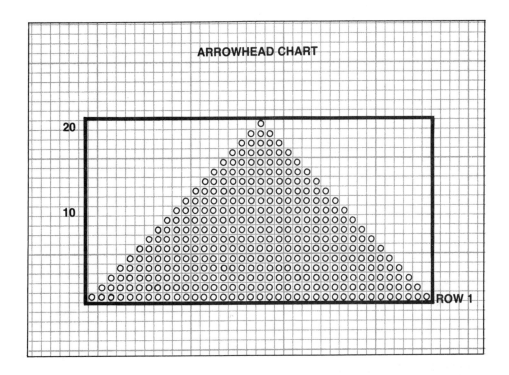

ARROWHEAD CHART

20

10

ROW 1

SLEEVES

With smaller needles and A, cast on 35 (35,37) sts. Work in k 1, p 1 ribbing for 2"/5cm; inc 1 st at end of last row. Change to larger needles and MC; inc 1 st each edge every 6th row until there are 52 (56,62) sts. At same time, when 10 MC rows are completed, mark center 6 sts; carry markers to end of sleeve. Continue in color pattern as follows: For 10 rows, work in MC to marker, work 6 sts in A, work MC to end. Work 10 rows MC. For next 10 rows, work in MC to marker, work 6 sts B, work MC to end. Work 10 rows MC. Working in pattern as established, when 16 (17,18)"/40.5 (43,45.5) cm from beg, end with right side facing.

SHAPE CAP

Keeping to color pattern, bind off 3 (2,4) sts at beg of next 2 rows, then dec 1 st each edge every other row 20 (23,24) times until 6 sts remain. Sl sts to holder for neckband.

FINISHING

Block pieces lightly. Sew left sleeve to front and back. Sew right sleeve to front. Neckband: With smaller needles and A, k across 27 sts from back neck holder, 6 sts from left sleeve, pick up and k 16 sts to front neck holder, k across 21 sts from front neck holder, pick up and k 16 sts up right front neck edge, k 6 sts from right sleeve. Work in k 1, p 1 ribbing for 1"/2.5cm. Bind off loosely in ribbing. Sew remaining raglan seam, including neckband. Sew side and sleeve seams.

PENCIL-STRIPED PULLOVER

AN OLD STANDARD, UPDATED IN BRIGHT COLORS AND A HEAVY WOOL YARN.

SIZES
Directions are for boy's small, with medium and large in parentheses. Finished chest measurements 36 (39,42)"/91.5 (99,106.5) cm; length to back neck edge 22 (24,26)"/56 (61,66) cm; armhole measures 13 (14,14½)"/33 (35.5,37) cm; length of sleeve from underarm 16 (17,18)"/40.5 (43,45.5) cm.

MATERIALS
14 (18,22) oz/400 (510,625) gr knitting worsted in royal blue (MC), 1oz/30gr each green (A), gold (B), red (C), denim (D)

NEEDLES
One pair each size 6/4mm and size 8/5mm needles, or size needed to obtain gauge. 6 stitch holders

GAUGE
4 sts and 6 rows = 1"/2.5cm on size 8 needles over st st

BACK
With smaller needles and MC, cast on 71 (77,83) sts. Work in k 1, p 1 ribbing for 2"/5cm. Inc 1 st at end of last row. Change to larger needles and st st and work in stripe pattern as follows: 12 (16,16) rows MC, 2 rows A, 26 (28,30) rows MC, 2 rows B,

26 (28,30) rows MC, 2 rows C, 28 (30,32) rows MC, 2 rows D, MC to end. Working pattern, when piece measures 14 (15,16)"/35.5 (38,40.5) cm from beg, end with right side facing.

SHAPE ARMHOLES

Continuing stripe pattern, bind off 4 sts at beg of next 2 rows, then 1 st each edge every other row 4 times. Work even until armhole measures 8 (9,10)″/20 (23,25.5) cm. Sl 16 (19,22) sts to holder for shoulder, 24 sts to holder for neckband, and rem 16 (19,22) sts to holder for other shoulder.

FRONT

Work as for back until 5 (6,7)″/12.5 (15,18) cm above beg of armhole shaping. End with right side facing.

SHAPE NECK

Mark center 16 sts. Work to first marker. With second strand, work to next marker, sl sts between markers to holder for neckband, work to end. Working both sides simultaneously, dec 1 st each neck edge every other row 4 times. Work even until same length as back to shoulders. Sl sts to holders for shoulders.

SLEEVES

With smaller needles and MC, cast on 35 (35,37) sts. Work in k 1, p 1 ribbing for 2″/5cm; inc 1 st at end of last row. Change to larger needles and work in stripe pattern as follows: 24 (28,28) rows MC, 2 rows A, 26 (28,30) rows MC, 2 rows B, 26 (28,30) rows MC, 2 rows C, 26 (28,30) 2 rows D, work to end with MC. At the same time, inc 1 st at each edge every 6th row until there are 52 (56,58) sts. When same number of rows above C stripe as on back, end with right side facing.

CAP SHAPING

Bind off 4 sts at beg of next 2 rows, then dec 1 st each edge every other row 4 times. Work even until 3½ (4,4¾)″/9 (10,12) cm from beg of cap shaping. Bind off 2 sts at beg of every row until 8 (8,6) sts rem. Bind off.

FINISHING

Block pieces lightly. Sew left shoulder seam. Neckband: With smaller needles and MC, k across 24 sts from back neck holder, pick up and k 21 sts to front neck holder, k across 16 sts from front neck holder, pick up and k 21 sts to shoulder. Work in k 1, p 1 ribbing for 1″/2.5cm. Bind off loosely in ribbing. Join right shoulder, including neckband. Sew in sleeves, matching C stripe. Sew side and sleeve seams, taking care to match stripes.

SUMMER MESH TOP

**WHAT TO WEAR WHEN THE WEATHER GETS HOT? THIS TOP
KEEPS YOU COVERED, BUT COOL.**

SIZE

Note: top is oversized for a blouson effect.
Directions are for girl's small, with medium and large
in parentheses. Finished chest measurements 45½
(49,53)"/115 (124.5,134.5) cm; length to back neck
edge 19 (21,23)"/48 (53.5,58.5) cm; armhole measures 14 (16,18)"/35.5 (40.5,45.5) cm; length of
sleeve to underarm 18 (19,20)"/45.5 (48,51) cm.

MATERIALS

10½ (12¼,14) oz/300 (350,400) gr sportweight
perle cotton

NEEDLES

One pair each size 6/4mm and size 8/5mm needles,
or size needed to obtain gauge
5 stitch holders

GAUGE

13 sts = 4"/10cm and 6 rows = 1"/2.5cm on size 8
needles over pattern

BACK

With smaller needles, cast on 73 (79,85) sts. Work in k 1, p 1 ribbing for 2"/5cm. Inc 1 st at end of last row. Change to larger needles and work pattern as follows: K 1, *yo, sl 1 as if to p, k 1, psso; repeat from *. Repeat this row for pattern until 12 (13,14)"/30.5 (33,35.5) cm from beg.

SHAPE ARMHOLES

Bind off 14 sts at beg of next 2 rows. Work even in pattern as established until 7 (8,9)"/18 (20,23) cm. Sl 9 (12,15) sts to holder for shoulder, 28 sts to holder for neck, and 9 (12,15) sts to holder for other shoulder.

FRONT

Work as for back until 1"/2.5cm above beg of armhole shaping.

SHAPE V-NECK

Mark center of row. Work to marker; with 2nd strand, work to end. Keeping to pattern as established, dec 1 st at each neck edge every other row until 9 (12,15) sts rem on each side. When same length as back to shoulder, sl sts to holder.

SLEEVES

With smaller needles, cast on 45 (51,57) sts. Work in k 1, p 1 ribbing for 1"/2.5cm. Inc 1 st at end of last row. Change to larger needles and work in pattern as for back until 18 (19,20)"/45.5 (48,51) cm from beg. Bind off.

FINISHING

Join left shoulder seam. With smaller needles, right side facing, k across 28 sts from back neck holder, pick up and k 37 (43,49) sts to center front, 1 st in center of V-neck, and 37 (43,49) sts to shoulder. Row 1: Beg with p, work in k 1, p 1 ribbing to 2 sts before center st, k 2 tog, p center st, k 2 tog, work in ribbing to end. Continue in k 1, p 1 ribbing, dec 1 st each side of center st, until 1"/2.5cm from beg. Bind off in ribbing. Join shoulder seam, including neckband. Sew in sleeves. Sew side and sleeve seams.

Fishnet Vest and Scarf

**When a T-shirt isn't enough, this vest will do the trick.
The matching scarf ties up hair, waist, whatever.**

VEST

Sizes
Directions are for girl's small, with medium and large in parentheses. Finished chest measurements 36 (37⅓,40)"/91.5 (95,101.5) cm; length to back neck edge 19⅓ (22,24⅓)"/49 (56,62) cm.

Materials
5 (7,7) oz/150 (200,200) gr light sportweight cotton blend

Crochet Hook
One size D/3.25mm crochet hook, or size needed to obtain gauge

Gauge
6 ch = 1"/2.5cm; 3 rows tr = 2"/5cm with size D hook

Back
Ch 115 (119,127).
Row 1: 1 tr in 11th ch from hook (10 ch count as 3 ch, 1 tr, ch 3), *ch 3, sk 3 ch, tr in next ch; rep from * across.
Row 2: Ch 7, turn (counts as first tr, ch 3); * tr in next tr, ch 3, sk 3 ch; repeat from * across; end sk 3 ch, tr in next ch.
Rep row 2 until 12 (14,16)"/30.5 (33.5,40.5) cm from beg.

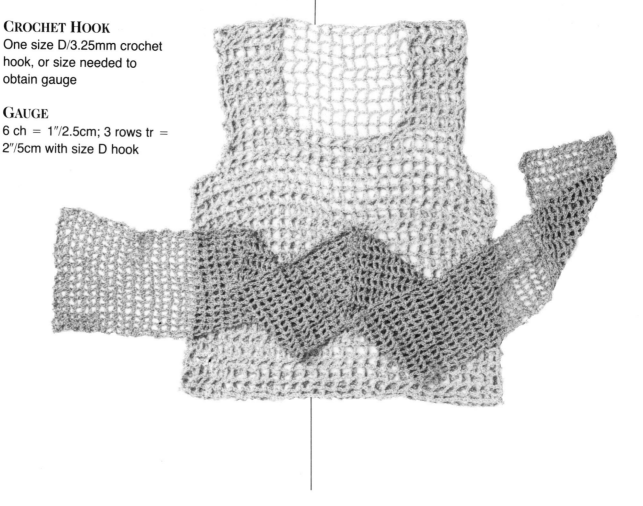

SHAPE ARMHOLES

Sl st until 4th (4th,5th) tr, continue as for row 2 until 4th (4th,5th) tr from end. Ch 7, turn. Continue as for row 2 until 11 (12,14) rows from beg of armhole shaping. Fasten off.

FRONT

Work as for back until 3 (3,4) rows above beg of armhole shaping.

SHAPE NECK

Work across until 7 squares are worked. Ch 7, turn. Continue in mesh pattern on 7 mesh until same length as back. Fasten off. Join yarn to other shoulder, working 7 mesh squares to correspond to first shoulder.

FINISHING

Sew shoulder and side seams.

SCARF

SIZES

One size fits all. Scarf measures 8"/20cm wide and 50"/127cm long.

MATERIALS

3½oz/100gr light sportweight cotton

CROCHET HOOK

One size D/3.5mm crochet hook, or size needed to obtain gauge

GAUGE

6 ch = 1"/2.5cm; 3 rows tr = 2"/5cm with size D hook

BACK

Ch 55.
Row 1: 1 tr in 11th ch from hook (10 ch count as 3 ch, 1 tr, ch 3), *ch 3, sk 3 ch, tr in next ch; rep from * across.
Row 2: Ch 7, turn (counts as first tr, ch 3); *tr in next tr, ch 3, sk 3 ch; repeat from * across; end sk 3 ch, tr in next ch.
Rep row 2 until 50"/127cm from beg or desired length. Fasten off.

Vertical-Striped V-neck

VERTICAL STRIPES IN GRADUATED SHADES OF MAROON ON A GRAY BACKGROUND CREATE AN UNUSUAL BUT STILL CLASSIC EFFECT.

SIZES
Directions are for boy's small, with medium and large in parentheses. Finished chest measurements 36 (39,42)"/91.5 (99,106.5) cm; length to back neck edge 22 (24,26)"/56 (61,66) cm; armhole measures 13 (14,14½)"/33 (35.5,37) cm; length of sleeve from underarm 16 (17,18)"/40.5 (43,45.5) cm.

MATERIALS
10½ (12¼,14) oz/300 (350,400) gr sport yarn in gray (MC), ½oz/15gr each blackberry (A) and plum wine (B) and 1oz/30gr burgundy (C).

NEEDLES
One pair each size 3/3.25mm and 5/3.75mm knitting needles, or size needed to obtain gauge
2 stitch holders

GAUGE
6 sts and 7 rows = 1"/2.5cm on size 5 needles over st st

BACK
With smaller needles and MC, cast on 107 (115,125) sts and work in k 1, p 1 ribbing for 15 rows. Inc 1 st at end of last row. Change to larger needles and work in st st until piece measures 14 (15,16)"/35.5 (38,40.5) cm from beg. End with right side facing.

SHAPE ARMHOLES
Bind off 6 (6,8) sts at the beg of the next 2 rows. Then dec 1 st each side every other row 4 times until 88 (96,102) sts rem. Work even until piece measures 22 (24,26)"/56 (61,66) cm from beg. End with right side facing.

SHAPE SHOULDERS
Bind off 7 (9,10) sts at beg of next 2 rows, then 8 (9,10) sts at beg of next 4 rows. Place rem 42 sts on holder.

FRONT
Work ribbing as for back. Change to larger needles and start pattern as follows: K 5 (8,7), k 1 and mark st, k 5 (5,6), k 1 and mark st, k 5 (5,6), k 1 and mark st, k 5 (5,6), k 1 and mark st, k 5 (5,6), k 1 and mark st, k 5 (5,6), k 1 and mark st, k 17 (19,20), k 1 and mark st, k 17 (19,20), k 1 and mark st, k 17 (19,20), k

1 and mark st, k 18 (17,20). Continue in pattern as established, until 14 (15,16)"/35.5 (38,40.5) cm from beg. End with right side facing.

SHAPE ARMHOLES
Keeping to pattern, bind off 6 (6,8) sts at the beg of the next 2 rows. Dec 1 st each edge every other row 4 times until 88 (96,102) sts rem. Work even until piece measures 16 (18,20)"/40.5 (45.5,51) cm from beg. End with right side facing.

SHAPE V-NECK
Keeping to pattern, k first 44 (48,51) sts; sl rem sts to holder. Working on left side only, dec 1 st at neck edge on next row, then every other row until 23 (27,30) sts rem. Work even until same length as back to beg of shoulder shaping. End with right side facing.

SHAPE SHOULDERS
From shoulder edge, bind off 7 (9,10) sts once, then 8 (9,10) sts twice. Wrong side facing, sl sts from holder to needle. Complete right side to correspond, reversing all shaping.

SLEEVES
With smaller needles and MC, cast on 55 (57,59) sts. Work in k 1, p 1 ribbing for 17 rows, inc 1 st at end of last row, 56 (58,60) sts. Change to larger needles and start pattern as follows: K 18 (19,20), k 1 and mark st, k 18, k 1 and mark st, k 18 (19,20). Inc 1 st each edge every 4th row twice. Continue to increase every 4th row, working inc sts in st st until there are 78 (84,88) sts. Keeping to pattern, work until sleeve measures 16 (17,18)"/40.5 (43,45.5) cm from beg. End with right side facing.

SHAPE CAP
Bind off 6 (6,8) sts at beg of next 2 rows, then dec 1 st each edge on next row, then every other row 3 times more. Work even until armhole measures 2 (2,3)"/5 (5,7.5) cm. End with right side facing. Bind off 2 sts at the beg of every row until 6 sts rem. Bind off.

NECKBAND
Sew left shoulder seam. With smaller needles and MC, from right side, k sts from back holder, pick up and k 49 sts to center front, pick up and k 1 st between 2 center sts and mark this st, pick up 49 sts to left shoulder; 139 sts. Work in k 1, p 1 ribbing to 2 sts before marked st, k 2 tog, k marked st, k 2 tog, work in ribbing to end. Keeping to ribbing as established, dec as before either side of center st every other row 2 times more. Bind off loosely in ribbing.

FINISHING
Sew right shoulder and neckband seam. Sew in sleeves, centering sleeves on shoulder seam. Beg on front with first marked st from right edge, work duplicate st (see Basic Knitting Techniques) up marked st to top edge in the following colors: C, C, C, B, A, B, A, B, A. Work sleeves in same manner, working stripes in C. Sew side and sleeve seams.

STAID PLAID

USING TWO SHADES OF GRAY MAKES THIS PLAID PATTERN SUBTLE ENOUGH FOR A BOY TO WEAR.

SIZES
Directions are for boy's small, with medium and large in parentheses. Finished chest measurements 37 (40,42)"/94 (101.5,106.5) cm; length to back neck edge 21 (23,25)"/53.5 (58.5,63.5) cm; armhole measures 14 (16,18)"/35.5 (40.5,45.5) cm; length of sleeve from underarm 18 (19,20)"/45.5 (48.5,51) cm.

MATERIALS
10½ (10½,14) oz/300 (300,400) gr knitting worsted in light gray (MC), 7oz/200gr medium gray (CC)

NEEDLES
One pair each size 6/4mm and 8/5mm needles, or size needed to obtain gauge
6 stitch holders
Size G/4.5mm crochet hook

GAUGE
4 sts and 6 rows = 1"/2.5cm on size 8 needles over st st

BACK
With smaller needles and CC, cast on 75 (81,85) sts. Work in k 1, p 1 ribbing for 2"/5cm. Change to larger needles, MC, and st st, and work in stripe pattern as follows: *10 rows MC, 2 rows CC. Repeat

from * until 14 (15,16)"/35.5 (38,40.5) cm from beg. End with right side facing.

SHAPE ARMHOLES
Bind off 2 sts at beg of next 2 rows. Continue in pattern until armhole measures 7 (8,9)"/18 (20,23) cm. End with right side facing. Sl 24 (26,27) sts to holder for right shoulder, 23 (25,27) sts to holder for neck, and rem 24 (26,27) sts to holder for left shoulder.

FRONT

Work as for back until 4 (5,6)"/10 (12.5,15) cm above beg of armhole shaping. End with right side facing.

SHAPE NECK

Mark center 19 (21,23) sts. Keeping to stripe pattern, work to first marker, join new strand, work to next marker, sl sts between markers to holder for neckband, work to end. Working both sides simultaneously, dec 1 st each edge every other row twice. Work even until same length as back to shoulders. Sl sts for each shoulder to holders.

SLEEVES

With smaller needles and CC, cast on 37 (39,41) sts. Work in k 1, p 1 ribbing for 2"/5cm. Change to larger needles and work in stripe pattern as for back. At same time, inc 1 st at each edge every 6th row until there are 57 (65,73) sts. Work even until 18 (19,20)"/45.5 (48,51) cm from beg. Bind off.

FINISHING

Block pieces lightly, omitting ribbings.

Vertical stripes: Beg on back, mark center st. Join CC at top of ribbing in stitch next to marked st, work ch stripe up st (see Basic Knitting Techniques), taking care to keep work flat. Work another ch stripe in st on other side of center st. Working out from center st to both edges, *sk 7 sts, work ch stripe in next st, skip next st, work ch stripe in next st; repeat from * to each edge.

Work front and sleeves in same manner, working inc sts on sleeves into pattern. Join left shoulder seam. Right side facing, with smaller needles and CC, k across 23 (25,27) sts from back neck holder, pick up and k 21 sts to front holder, k 19 (21,23) sts from holder, pick up and k 21 sts to right shoulder. Work in k 1, p 1 ribbing for 2½"/6cm. Join right shoulder and neckband seam. Turn neckband to inside and sew loosely in place. Center sleeves and sew in place. Sew side and sleeve seams.

MAD PLAID

THE COLORS IN THIS PULLOVER REALLY BOUNCE! THREE-QUARTER-LENGTH SLEEVES ARE DONE IN REVERSE COLORS.

SIZES

Directions are for girl's small, with medium and large in parentheses. Finished chest measurements 36 (38,41)"/91.5 (96.5,104) cm; length to back neck edge 20 (22,24)"/51 (56,61) cm; armhole measures 12 (14,16)"/30.5 (35.5,40.5) cm; length of sleeve from underarm 11 (12,13)"/28 (30.5,33) cm.

MATERIALS

10½ (10½,14) oz/300 (300,400) gr knitting worsted in magenta (MC), 7 (7,10½)"/200 (200,300) gr blue (CC)

NEEDLES

One pair each size 6/4mm and size 8/5mm needles, or size needed to obtain gauge
6 stitch holders
Size G/4.5mm crochet hook

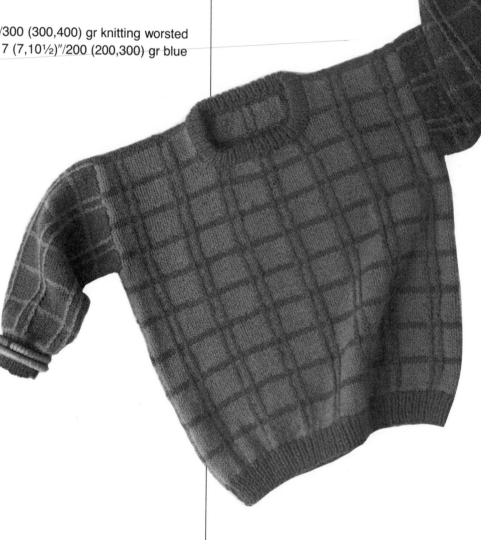

GAUGE

4 sts and 6 rows = 1"/2.5cm on size 8 needles over st st

BACK

With smaller needles and CC, cast on 73 (77,83) sts. Work in k 1, p 1 ribbing for 2"/5cm. Change to larger needles, MC, and st st, and work in stripe pattern as follows: *10 rows MC, 2 rows CC. Repeat from * until 14 (15,16)"/35.5 (38,40.5) cm from beg. End with right side facing.

SHAPE ARMHOLES

Bind off 2 sts at beg of next 2 rows. Continue in pattern until armhole measures 6 (7,8)"/15 (18,20) cm. End with right side facing. Sl 23 (24,26) sts to holder for right shoulder, 23 (25,27) sts to holder for neck, and rem 23 (24,26) sts to holder for left shoulder.

FRONT

Work as for back until armhole measures 3 (4,5)"/7.5 (10,12.5) cm. End with right side facing.

SHAPE NECK

Mark center 19 (21,23) sts. Keeping to stripe pattern, work to first marker, join new strand, work to next marker, sl sts between markers to holder for neckband, work to end. Working both sides simultaneously, dec 1 st each neck edge every other row twice. Work even until same length as back to shoulders. Sl sts for each shoulder to holders.

SLEEVES

With smaller needles and CC, cast on 41 (45,49) sts. Work in k 1, p 1 ribbing for 2"/5cm. Change to larger needles and work in stripe pattern as follows: 2 rows MC, 10 rows CC. At same time, inc 1 st at each edge every 6th row until there are 49 (57,65) sts. Work even until 11 (12,13)"/28 (30.5,33) cm from beg for ¾-length sleeves. Bind off.

FINISHING

Block pieces lightly, omitting ribbings.

Vertical stripes: Beg on back, mark center st. Join CC at top of ribbing in stitch next to marked st, work ch stripe up st (see Basic Knitting Techniques), taking care to keep work flat. Work another ch stripe in st on other side of center st. Working out from center st to both edges, *sk 7 sts, work ch stripe in next st, skip next st, work ch stripe in next st; repeat from * to each edge.

Work front in same manner. Work sleeves in same manner, working ch stripes with MC. Join left shoulder seam. With right side facing, smaller needles, and CC, k across 23 (25,27) sts from back neck holder, pick up and k 19 sts to front holder, k 19 (21,23) sts from holder, pick up and k 19 sts to right shoulder. Work in k 1, p 1 ribbing for 2"/5cm. Bind off loosely in ribbing. Join right shoulder, including neckband seam. Turn neckband to inside and sew loosely in place. Sew in sleeves, centering sleeves on shoulders. Sew side and sleeve seams.

CRAYON HORIZONTAL VEST

**CRAYON COLORS ON WHITE IN A SPORTWEIGHT, EASY-CARE
YARN WILL BRIGHTEN ANY OUTFIT.**

SIZES

Directions are for girl's small, with medium and large in parentheses. Finished chest measurements 35 (37,40)"/86.5 (94,101.5) cm, length to back neck edge 21¼ (22½,24¼)"/54 (57,61.5) cm.

MATERIALS

7 (8¾,10½) oz/200 (250,300) gr sportweight in white (MC), 1oz/30gr each maize (A), blue (B), red (C), green (D)

NEEDLES

One pair each size 3/3.25mm and size 5/3.75mm needles, or size needed to obtain gauge
2 stitch holders

GAUGE

6 sts and 7 rows = 1"/2.5cm on size 5 needles over st st

BACK

With smaller needles and MC, cast on 105 (111,119) sts. Work in k 1, p 1 ribbing for 2"/5cm. Inc 1 st at end of last row. Change to larger needles and st st and work 16 (18,20) rows MC. Continue in st st and work stripe pattern as follows: 2 rows A, 28 (30,32) rows MC, 2 rows B, 28 (30,32) rows MC, 2 rows C, 28 (30,32) rows MC, 2 rows D, MC to

end. At same time, when piece measures 14¼ (15,16¼)"/36 (38,41) cm from beg, end with right side facing.

SHAPE ARMHOLES
Bind off 6 (6,8) sts at beg of next 2 rows, then 2 sts at beg of next 4 rows. Continue in pattern until armhole measures 7 (7½,8)"/18 (19,20.5) cm. End with right side facing.

SHAPE SHOULDERS
Bind off 7 (8,8) sts at beg of next 4 rows, then 7 (8,10) sts at beg of next 2 rows. Sl rem 44 sts to holder for neckband.

FRONT
Work as for back until 6 (8,10) rows above D stripe. End with right side facing.

SHAPE NECK
Mark center 28 sts. Work to first marker, with second strand, work to next marker, sl sts between markers to holder for neckband, work to end. Working both sides simultaneously, dec 1 st each neck edge every other row until 21 (24,26) sts remain. Work even until same length as back to shoulders. Bind off from each outside edge as for back.

FINISHING
Block pieces lightly. Sew left shoulder seam. Neckband: With smaller needles and MC, k across 44 sts from back neck holder, pick up and k 23 sts to front neck holder, k across 28 sts from front neck holder, pick up and k 23 sts to shoulder. Work in k 1, p 1 ribbing for 1¼"/3cm. Bind off loosely in ribbing. Sew right shoulder seam, including neckband. Armbands: Right side facing, with smaller needles and MC, pick up and k 79 (85,93) sts along armhole edge and work in k 1, p 1 ribbing for 1¼"/3 cm. Bind off loosely in ribbing. Sew side seams, including armbands.

SPORTY STRIPES

VERTICAL STRIPES IN SIMILAR COLORS TO THE HORIZONTAL
VERSION WILL REMIND YOU OF A REFEREE'S SHIRT—
BUT THIS IS SO MUCH MORE FUN.

SIZES
Directions are for boy's small, with medium and large in parentheses. Finished chest measurements 36 (39,42)"/91.5 (99,106.5) cm; length to back neck edge 22 (24,26)"/58.5 (63.5,68.5) cm.

MATERIALS
8¾ (10½,12¼) oz/250 (300,350) gr sport yarn in white (MC), 1/2oz/15gr each green (A), blue (B), and red (C).

NEEDLES
One pair each size 3/3.25mm and 5/3.75mm knitting needles, or size needed to obtain gauge
2 stitch holders

GAUGE
6 sts and 7 rows = 1"/2.5cm on size 5 needles over st st

BACK
With smaller needles and MC, cast on 107 (115,125) sts and work in k 1, p 1 ribbing for 15 rows. Inc 1 st at end of last row. Change to larger needles and work in st st until piece measures 14 (15,16)"/35.5 (38,40.5) cm from beg. End with right side facing.

SHAPE ARMHOLES
Bind off 6 (6,8) sts at beg of next 2 rows. Then dec 1 st each side every other row 4 times until 88 (96,102) sts rem. Work even until piece measures 22 (24,26)"/56 (61,66) cm from beg. End with right side facing.

▲ CAMOUFLAGE-AND-SUEDE PULLOVER

► **PEPLUMED DIAMONDS** (left)

GLITTERY DIAMONDS (right)

▼ **PENCIL-STRIPED PULLOVER**

▲ COTTON GUERNSEY (left)

SUMMER MESH TOP (right)

▶ FISHNET VEST AND SCARF

▼ **SPORTY STRIPES** (left)

CRAYON HORIZONTAL VEST (right)

▶ **FAIR ISLE VEST AND MATCHING TIE**

▲ **SNOWFLAKE RAGG PULLOVER AND SKI HAT** (left)

VERTICAL-STRIPED V-NECK (right)

STAID PLAID (left)

◄ **MAD PLAID** (right)

◄ BALLERINA VEST AND LEGWARMERS

▲ FEMININE FAIR ISLE SWEATER SET (left)

BOUCLE PULLOVER JACKET AND CLOCHE (right)

▲ JUNGLE PRINT

▶ SILK BLEND TUNICS

▼ **ICELANDIC PULLOVER** (right)

GIRL'S ICELANDIC OUTERWEAR (center)

BOY'S ICELANDIC VEST AND HAT (left)

◄ **COLORED COTTONS**

▼ **FRENCH SAILOR SHIRT** (left)

ARROW RAGLAN (right)

SHAPE SHOULDERS

Bind off 7 (9,10) sts at beg of next 2 rows, then 8 (9,10) sts at beg of next 4 rows. Place rem 42 sts on holder.

FRONT

Work ribbing as for back for 14 rows; p next row, inc 1 st at end of row. Change to larger needles and start pattern as follows: K 5 (8,7), k 1 and mark st, k 5 (5,6), k 1 and mark st, k 5 (5,6), k 1 and mark st, k 5 (5,6), k 1 and mark st, k 5 (5,6), k 1 and mark st, k 17 (19,20), k 1 and mark st, k 17 (19,20), k 1 and mark st, k 18 (17,20). Do not carry markers. Work even in st st until 14 (15,16)"/35.5 (38,40.5) cm from beg. End with right side facing.

SHAPE ARMHOLES

Keeping to pattern, bind off 6 (6,8) sts at the beg of the next 2 rows. Dec 1 st each edge every other row 4 times until 88 (96,102) sts rem. Work even until piece measures 16 (18,20)"/40.5 (45.5,51) cm from beg. End with right side facing.

SHAPE V-NECK

Keeping to pattern, k first 44 (48,51) sts; sl rem sts to holder. Working on left side only, dec 1 st at neck edge on next row, then every other row until 23 (27,30) sts rem. Work even until same length as back to beg of shoulder shaping. End with right side facing.

SHAPE SHOULDER

From shoulder edge, bind off 7 (9,10) sts once, then 8 (9,10) sts twice. Wrong side facing, sl sts from holder to needle. Complete right side to correspond, reversing all shaping.

NECKBAND

Sew left shoulder seam. With smaller needles and MC, from right side, k sts from back holder, pick up and k 49 sts to center front, pick up and k 1 st between 2 center sts and mark this st, pick up 49 sts to left shoulder, 141 sts. Work in k 1, p 1 ribbing to 2 sts before marked st, k 2 tog, k marked st, k 2 tog, work in ribbing to end. Keeping to ribbing as established, dec as before either side of center st every other row 2 times more. Bind off loosely in ribbing.

FINISHING

Block pieces, omitting ribbings. Sew right shoulder seam, including neckband. Beg on right front with first marked st from right edge, work in duplicate st (see Basic Knitting Techniques) up marked st to top edge in the following colors: C, C, C, B, A, B, A, B, A. Armbands: Right side facing, with smaller needles and MC, pick up and k 125 (139,156) sts along armhole edge. Work in k 1, p 1 ribbing for 1"/2.5cm. Bind off loosely in ribbing. Sew side and armband seams.

FAIR ISLE VEST AND MATCHING TIE

**THE BORDER AT THE NECK ADDS JUST THE RIGHT
AMOUNT OF DETAIL TO THIS FINE-KNIT VEST OF SHETLAND WOOL.
NOT TOO FUSSY FOR THE MOST MASCULINE OF BOYS.**

VEST

SIZES
Directions are for boy's small, with medium and large in parentheses. Finished chest measurements 36 (39,42½)"/91.5 (99,108) cm; length to back neck edge 19 (21,23)"/48 (53.5,58.5) cm.

MATERIALS
7 (8,10) oz/200 (230,285) gr Shetland wool in evergreen (MC), and ½oz/15gr each cinnabar (A) and light gold (B)

NEEDLES
One pair each size 2/2.75mm and size 4/3.5mm needles, or size needed to obtain gauge
1 size 2/2.75mm circular needle
1 stitch holder

GAUGE
13 sts = 2"/2.5cm; 8 rows = 1"/2.5cm on size 4 needles over st st

BACK
With smaller needles and MC, cast on 117 (127, 137) sts. Work in k 1, p 1 ribbing for 2"/5cm. Inc 1 st at end of last row. Change to larger needles and st st and work even until 12 (13,14)"/30.5 (33,35.5) cm from beg. End with right side facing.

SHAPE ARMHOLES
Bind off 8 sts at beg of next 2 rows, then 2 sts at beg of next 4 rows. Work even until armhole measures 7 (8,9)"/18 (20,23) cm. End with right side facing.

SHAPE SHOULDERS
Bind off 10 (12,14) sts at beg of next 4 rows, then 10 (11,12) sts at beg of next 2 rows. Sl rem 34 sts to holder for neckband.

FRONT
Work as for back until armhole measures 1"/2.5cm. End with right side facing.

SHAPE V-NECK
Mark center 8 sts. Keeping to st st, work to first marker; with new strand, bind off to next marker, work to end. Working both sides simultaneously, dec 1 st at each neck edge on next row, then every other row until 30 (35,40) sts rem. Work even until same length as back to beg of shoulders. Bind off from each outside edge as for back.

FINISHING

Block pieces lightly. Sew shoulder seams. Neckband: With circular needle and MC, right side facing, beg at right side of neck edge and pick up and k 57 (65,73) sts to right shoulder, k across 34 sts from back neck holder, pick up and k 57 (65,73) sts along left neck edge (do not pick up sts in bound-off sts at center front). Working back and forth on circular needle, p 1 row. Drop MC; with A and B, follow chart for 6 rows. Fasten off A and B. With MC, k 1 row. Work 1 row k 1, p 1 ribbing. Bind off loosely in ribbing. Sew ends of neckband to bound-off sts of front, then sew bound-off edges of neckband tog for ¾"/2cm from bottom of V-neck. Gently steam press neckline edge. Armbands: With smaller needles and MC, right side facing, pick up and k 129 (145,161) sts along armhole edge. Work in k 1, p 1 ribbing for ¾"/2cm. Bind off loosely in ribbing. Sew side and armband seams.

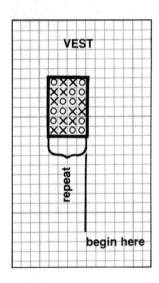

KEY:

☒ = A (cinnabar)
☐ (with O) = B (light gold)

TIE

MATERIALS

4oz/115gr Shetland wool in evergreen (MC), 1oz/30gr each cinnabar (A), light gold (B), and harvest gold (C).

NEEDLES

1 set size 4/3.5mm double-pointed knitting needles

GAUGE

13 sts = 2"/5cm; 8 rows = 1"/2.5cm on size 4 needles in st st

With MC, cast 16 sts onto first needle, 8 sts each on 2nd and 3rd needles, 32 sts in all. Taking care not to twist sts, join, and p 3 rnds. Continue in st st (k each rnd), work in pattern following chart until 21½"/54.5 cm from beg; fasten off A, B, and C. Continue with MC for 2 rnds. Dec rnd: On first needle, k 1, k 2 tog, k to last 3 sts on needle, k 2 tog, k 1; on 2nd needle, k 1, k 2 tog, k to end; on 3rd needle, k to last 3 sts, k 2 tog, k 1. *K 3 rnds. Repeat dec rnd. Repeat from * once, 20 sts. Work even in MC and st st until 33"/84cm above end of charted pattern. P 2 rnds. Bind off all sts in p.

FINISHING

Steam press lightly.

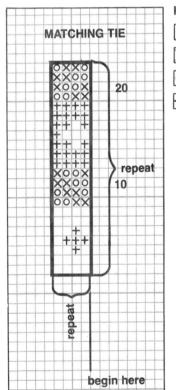

KEY:

☐ = MC (evergreen)
☒ = A (cinnabar)
☐ (with O) = B (light gold)
⊞ = C (harvest gold)

JUNGLE PRINT

THIS SWEATER WAS INSPIRED BY SWATCHES OF FABRIC MY BROTHER
BROUGHT BACK FROM AFRICA. THE COMBINATION OF BLACK AND WHITE
WITH VIBRANT COLORS MAKES IT A REAL STANDOUT.

SIZES

Directions are for girl's small, with medium and large
in parentheses. Finished chest measurements 34½
(37,39⅓)"/87 (94,100) cm; length to back neck edge
26 (27¼,28½)"/66 (69,72.5) cm; armhole measures
14¾ (17¼,19⅔)"/37.5 (44,50) cm; length of sleeve
from underarm 18⅔"/47.5cm (same for all sizes).

MATERIALS

5¼ (5¼,7) oz/150 (150,200) gr lightweight sport
yarn in black (MC), 3½ (3½,5¼) oz/100 (100,150)
gr white (CC), 1¾oz/50gr each hot pink (A), red (B),
and turquoise (C), and 3½oz/100gr menthe (D)

NEEDLES

One pair 32"/81cm circular needles, sizes 2/2.75mm
and 3/3.25mm, or size needed
to obtain gauge
One set each size
2/2.75mm and size
3/3.25mm double-pointed
needles

GAUGE

13 sts and 15 rows or rnds =
2"/5cm on size 3 needles in color
pattern

BODY

With smaller circular needle and MC, cast on 224
(240,256) sts. Taking care not to twist sts, join and
work around in k 1, p 1 ribbing for 1"/2.5cm. Mark
beg of rnd; carry marker. Change to larger circular
needle and st st, and begin color pattern: work chart
I twice, chart II once, chart III once, chart II once.
Work 4 rnds of chart I.

DIVIDE FOR BACK AND FRONT

Keeping to 5th rnd of chart I, work 112 (120,128) sts
for front and sl to holder. Turn. Working back and
forth on circular needle, continue to repeat chart I
until 6 (7¼,8½)"/15 (18.5,21.5) cm above dividing
row, ending with a p row. With MC, work in k 1, p 1
ribbing for 1"/2.5cm. Bind off in ribbing. Sl sts for
front to needle and complete as for back.

SLEEVES

With smaller dp needle and MC, cast on 96
(112,128) sts, evenly divided on 3 needles. Taking
care not to twist sts, join and work in k 1, p 1 ribbing
for 1"/2.5cm. Mark beg of rnd; carry markers.
Change to larger needle and st st, and work chart I
twice, chart II once, chart III once, chart II once. Bind
off all sts.

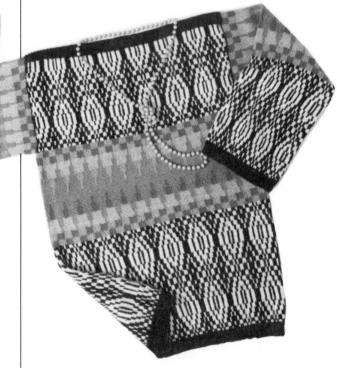

FINISHING

Block lightly, omitting ribbings. Sew shoulder seams, leaving approximately 8"/20cm open for neck. Sew in sleeves, easing to fit. Steam seams lightly.

CHART II

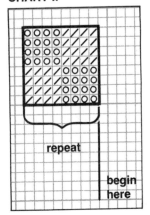

repeat

begin here

CHART I

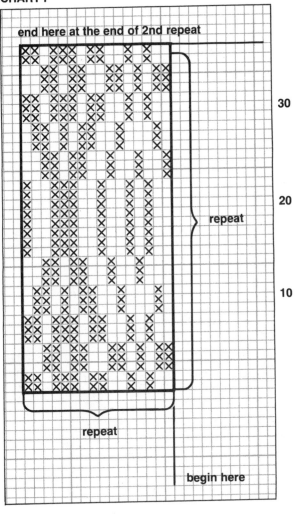

end here at the end of 2nd repeat

30

20

repeat

10

repeat

begin here

CHART III

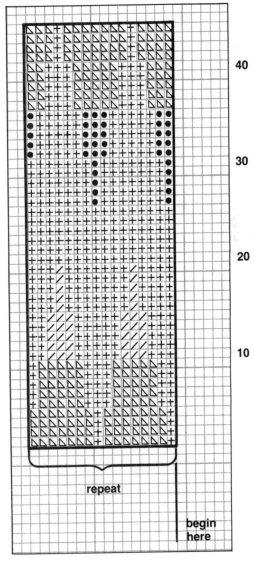

40

30

20

10

repeat

begin here

KEY:

☒ = MC (black)

= CC (white)

⦿ = A (hot pink)

◿ = B (red)

◺ = C (turquoise)

⊞ = D (menthe)

FRENCH SAILOR SHIRT

THIS IS A MODERN REVISION OF A FRENCH SAILOR'S SHIRT. I'VE ADDED TOUCHES OF RED HERE AND THERE FOR A MORE AMERICAN LOOK.

SIZES

Directions are for girl's small, with medium and large in parentheses. Finished chest measurements 36 (38,40)"/91.5 (96.5,101) cm; length to back neck edge 25 (27,29)"/63.5 (68.5,73.5) cm; armhole measures 14 (16,18)"/35.5 (40.5,45.5) cm; length of sleeve from underarm 12"/30.5cm (the same for all sizes).

MATERIALS

12¼ (14,15¾) oz/350 (400,450) gr sportweight mercerized cotton in white (MC)
3oz/85gr each red (A) and royal blue (B)
3 red star appliqués
or buttons (optional)

NEEDLES

One pair each size 4/3.5mm and size 6/4mm needles, or size needed to obtain gauge
5 stitch holders

GAUGE

11 sts = 2"/5cm and 7 rows = 1"/2.5cm on size 6 needles over st st

BACK

Note: When changing colors, be sure to pick up new color from under color just worked to prevent holes.

With larger needles and A, cast on 99 (105,111) sts. Work in garter st for 6 rows. Next row: K 6 sts A, with MC k across until 6 sts remain, with new strand of A, k to end. Keeping edge sts in A and garter st, and center sts in st st, work stripe pattern on center sts as follows: 11 more rows MC, *2 rows B, 12 rows MC; repeat from *. When 4"/10cm from beg, fasten off A and work across all sts in stripe pattern. Work even until 18 (19,20)"/45.5 (48,51) cm from beg. End with right side facing.

SHAPE ARMHOLES

Keeping to pattern, bind off 11 sts at beg of next 2 rows. Work even in pattern until armhole measures 7 (8,9)"/18 (20,23) cm. Sl 21 (24,27) sts to holder for shoulder, 35 sts to holder for back neck, sl rem sts to holder for shoulder.

FRONT

Work as for back until armhole measures 2"/5cm. End with right side facing.

SHAPE V-NECK

Mark center st. Keeping to st st and stripe pattern, work to marked st, sl center st to pin for neckband, with new strand work to end. Working both sides simultaneously, dec 1 st at each neck edge on next row, then every other row until 21 (24,27) sts rem.

Work even until same length as back to beg of shoulders. Sl sts to holders for shoulders.

SLEEVES

With larger needles and A, cast on 56 (60,66) sts. Work in garter st for 6 rows. Fasten off A. Continue in stripe pattern and st st for back. At same time, inc 1 st at each edge every other row until there are 76 (88,98) sts. Work even until 10"/25.5cm from beg. End with right side facing. Fasten off MC and B. With A, work in garter st for 2"/5cm. Bind off.

FINISHING

Block pieces lightly. Join left shoulder seam by knitted seam method. Neckband: Right side facing, with smaller needles and A, k across sts of back neck, pick up and k 38 (45,52) sts to center st, k center st, pick up and k 38 (45,52) sts to right shoulder. Working in garter st, work until 2 sts before center st, k 2 tog, k center st, k 2 tog, work to end. Continue in garter st, working dec on either side of center st, and sl center st every other row, for 1"/2.5 cm. Bind off. Join right shoulder, including neckband seam. Sew in sleeves, easing to fit, and sewing sides of A garter st rows at top of sleeve to bound-off sts of armhole shaping. Sew side and sleeve seams, taking care to match stripes. Sew stars to front as shown in photograph.

Snowflake Ragg Pullover and Ski Hat

**A COZY, UPDATED VERSION OF THE TRADITIONAL SNOWFLAKE SKI SWEATER.
THE RAGG BACKGROUND GIVES IT A COUNTRY FEELING.**

PULLOVER

SIZES

Directions are for boy's small, with medium and large in parentheses. Finished chest measurements 37 (40,42)"/94 (101.5,106.5) cm; length to back neck edge 24 (26,28½)"/61 (66,72.5) cm; armhole measures 13 (14½,15½)"/33 (37,39) cm; length of sleeve from underarm 15 (16,17½)"/38 (40.5; 44.5) cm.

MATERIALS

20 (20,24) oz/570 (570,680) gr knitting worsted in ragg-type gray (MC), and 2oz/60gr each indigo (A) and garnet (B)

NEEDLES

One pair each size 6/4mm and size 8/5mm needles, or size needed to obtain gauge
4 stitch holders
bobbins (optional)

GAUGE

4 sts and 5 rows = 1"/2.5cm on size 8 needles over st st

BACK

Note: When changing colors, take up new color under color just worked to prevent holes. Carry unused yarn loosely across back of work, taking care to keep work flat. If desired, snowflakes can be worked with bobbins, and small patterns can be worked in duplicate stitch later.

With smaller needles and MC, cast on 73 (79,83) sts. Work in k 1, p 1 ribbing for 2"/5cm. Inc 1 st at end of last row. Change to larger needles and work 2 rows in st st. Keeping to st st, work chart I, then work even in MC until 12½ (14½,15½)"/32 (37,39.5) cm. End with right side facing. Work chart II; at same time, when 15 (17,18)"/38 (43,45.5) cm from beg and wrong side facing, begin armhole shaping.

CHART I

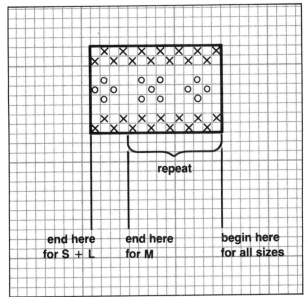

end here
for S + L

end here
for M

begin here
for all sizes

repeat

KEY:

☐ = MC (gray)

☒ = A (indigo)

◯ = B (garnet)

SHAPE RAGLAN ARMHOLES

Keeping to chart II, bind off 2 sts at beg of next 2 rows, then dec 1 st each edge every other row until 30 sts rem, continuing in MC when chart II is completed. Sl 30 sts to holder for neckband.

FRONT

Work as for back until armhole measures 5 (6,7)"/12.5 (15,18) cm. End with right side facing.

SHAPE NECK

Mark center 14 sts. Continuing raglan shaping, work to first marker, with second strand, work to next marker, sl sts between markers to holder for neckband, work to end. Working both sides simultaneously, dec 1 st each neck edge every other row, continuing raglan dec, until there are 2 sts rem. K 2 tog. Fasten off.

CHART II

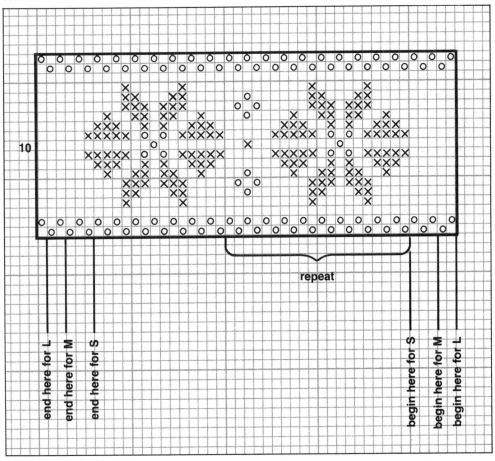

10

end here for L

end here for M

end here for S

repeat

begin here for S

begin here for M

begin here for L

CHART III

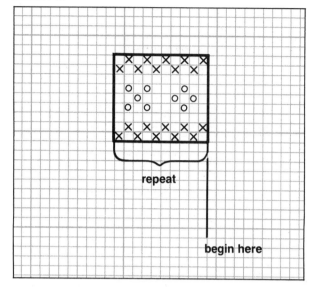

repeat

begin here

KEY:

☐ = MC (gray)

☒ = A (indigo)

Ⓞ = B (garnet)

SLEEVES

With smaller needles and MC, cast on 39 sts.
Work in k 1, p 1 ribbing for 2″/5cm, increasing 1 st at
end of last row. Change to larger needles. Inc row:
*k 2 in next st, k 3; repeat from * across—50 sts. P 1
row. Keeping to st st, work chart III, then continue in
MC, inc 1 st each edge every 4th row until there are
52 (58,62) sts. When sleeve measures 12½
(13½,15)″/32 (34,38) cm, beg chart IV. When sleeve
measures 15 (16,17½)″/38 (40.5,44.5) cm, end with
right side facing.

RAGLAN SHAPING

Keeping to chart, then continuing with MC, bind off 2
sts at beg of next 2 rows, then dec 1 st each edge
every other row until 8 sts rem. Sl sts to holder for
neckband.

CHART IV

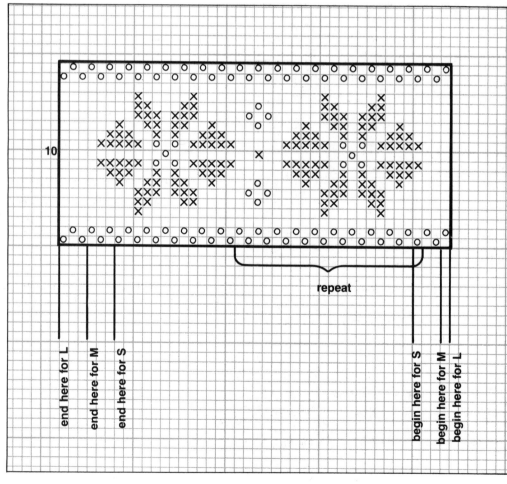

repeat

end here for L

end here for M

end here for S

begin here for S

begin here for M

begin here for L

FINISHING

Block pieces lightly. Neckband: With smaller needles and MC, right side facing, k across 30 sts from back neck holder, k 8 sts from left sleeve, pick up and k 9 (9,11) sts to front neck holder, k across 14 sts from front neck holder, pick up and k 9 (9,11) sts up neck edge, k 8 sts from right sleeve. Work in k 1, p 1 ribbing for 2½"/6cm. Bind off loosely in ribbing. Weave raglan, neckband seams, side and sleeve seams, taking care to match patterns. Turn neckband inward and loosely tack in place.

SKI HAT

SIZES

Directions are for small, with medium and large in parentheses. Finished measurements 21½ (22½,23½)"/54.5 (57,59.5) cm in diameter.

MATERIALS

4oz/115gr knitting worsted in ragg-type gray (MC), and 1oz/30gr each indigo (A) and garnet (B)

NEEDLES

One pair size 8/5mm needles, or size needed to obtain gauge.
One pair size 8/5mm double-pointed needles

GAUGE

4 sts and 5 rows = 1"/2.5cm on size 8 needles over st st

Note: When changing colors, take up new color under color just worked to prevent holes. Carry unused yarn loosely across back of work, taking care to keep work flat.

With MC, cast on 86 (90,94) sts. Work in st st for 3"/7.5cm; k 1 row on wrong side for turning ridge. Continue in st st for 5 rows, then work pattern following chart. Continue in st st with MC until 7 (8,9)"/18 (20,23) cm from turning ridge. End with right side

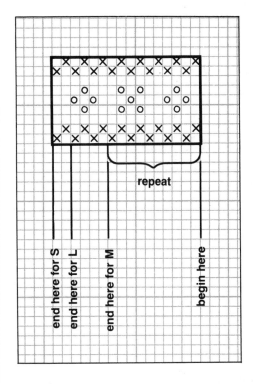

KEY:

☐ = MC (gray)

☒ = A (indigo)

☐(O) = B (garnet)

facing. Dividing row: Work first 43 (45,47) sts; with 2nd strand, work to end. Working each half separately, bind off 2 sts on each half at beg of next 8 rows. Sl each half to a dp needle.

FINISHING

Weave sts from dp needles; sew ends of top seam. Sew back seam. Turn hem to wrong side and sew in place.

BOUCLE PULLOVER JACKET AND CLOCHE

A WONDERFULLY SLOUCHY PULLOVER JACKET THAT LOOKS LIKE A TECHNICOLOR LAMB'S COAT.
DRESSMAKING TECHNIQUES ADD THE FINISHING TOUCHES.

PULLOVER JACKET

SIZES

Directions are for girl's small, with medium and large in parentheses. Finished chest measurements 37 (39,43)"/97 (99,109) cm; length to back neck edge 25½ (27,29)"/65 (68.5,73.5) cm; armhole measures 17 (18,20)"/43 (45.5,51) cm; length of sleeve from underarm 18 (19,20)"/45.5 (48,51) cm.

MATERIALS

21 (24½,26½) oz/600 (700,750) gr bulky boucle yarn (MC), 3½ (5¼,5¼) oz/100 (150,150) gr bulky weight yarn (CC)
4 pound-in snap fasteners ¼ yd/23cm finely knit stretch fabric for pocket linings

NEEDLES

One pair each size 8/5mm and 10/6mm knitting needles, or size needed to obtain gauge 1 stitch holder

GAUGE

4 sts = 1"/2.5cm and 9 rows = 2"/5cm on size 10 needles over reverse st st

BACK

With smaller needles and CC, cast on 73 (77,85) sts and work in k 1, p 1 ribbing for 13 rows. Inc 1 st at end of last row. Change to larger needles and MC, and work in reverse st st until 1"/2.5cm above ribbing. Keeping to reverse st st, cast on 2 sts at beg of next 2 rows for pocket extension. Work even until 6"/15cm from inc row. Bind off 2 sts at beg of next 2 rows. Continue to work even in reverse st st until piece measures 17 (18,19)"/43 (45.5,48) cm from beg. End with right side facing.

SHAPE ARMHOLES

Bind off 4 (4,5) sts at beg of the next 2 rows. Work even until piece measures 25½ (27,29)"/65 (68.5,73.5) cm from beg. End with right side facing.

SHAPE SHOULDERS

Bind off 20 (22,24) sts at the beg of next 2 rows. Place rem 26 (26,28) sts on holder.

FRONT

Work as for back until 16 (17,18)"/40.5 (43,45.5) cm from beg. End with right side facing. Change to CC and work 25 (26,28) sts in garter st, sl last 17 sts just knitted to a holder for pocket ribbing. With new strand of CC, cast on 17 sts on left needle. Working on these new sts, k 1, *p 1, k 1; repeat from * 7 times; k across rem sts. Keeping to patterns as established, working in garter st, and keeping 17 sts of pocket facing in k 1, p 1 ribbing, work even for 5 more rows. Mark center 4 sts. Drop CC. Join MC and continue in reverse st st.

SHAPE NECK AND ARMHOLES

Bind off 4 (4,5) sts, p across to first marker, bind off 4 sts to next marker; with new strand of yarn, p to end. Working both sides simultaneously, bind off 4 (4,5) sts at beg of next row, then work even in reverse st st until armhole measures 5½ (6,7)"/14 (15,18) cm. End with right side facing. From each neck edge, k 4 sts once and sl to holder, then dec 1 st at each neck edge every row until 20 (22,24) sts rem. Work even until same length as back to shoulder. Bind off.

SLEEVES

With smaller needles and CC, cast on 33 (35,41) sts. Work in k 1, p 1 ribbing for 13 rows, inc 1 st at end of last row—34 (36,42) sts. Change to larger needles, MC, and reverse st st, *k 1, inc 1 st in next st; repeat from * across—51 (54,63) sts. Continuing in reverse st st, inc 1 st each edge every 6th row 9 times—69 (72,81) sts. Work even until 18 (19,20)"/ 45.5 (48,51) cm from beg. Bind off all sts.

NECKBAND

Make 2. With smaller needles and CC, cast on 4 sts. Work in garter st until piece measures 5½ (6,7)"/14 (15,18) cm from beg when slightly stretched. Sl sts to holder. Sew garter st pieces to front neck edges, with sts on holders even with 4 bound-off sts. Sew shoulder seams. With smaller needles and MC, from right side, k sts from right holder, pick up and k 16 sts to shoulder seam, k 26 (26,28) sts from back holder, pick up and k 16 sts to front holder, k 4 sts from holder, pick up 48 sts to left shoulder—66 (66,68) sts. Work in garter st for 1"/2.5cm. Bind off loosely in k.

ARMHOLE TRIM

With smaller needles and CC, from right side, pick up and k 81 (85,89) sts around side of armhole edge from first st after bound-off sts to last st after bound-off sts. Work even in garter st until 1"/2.5cm from beg. Bind off loosely in garter st. Sew sides of garter st band to bound-off sts of armhole shaping.

POCKET TRIM

Sl sts from holders to smaller needle. With CC, work in k 1, p 1 ribbing for 1"/2.5cm. Bind off loosely in ribbing. Sew sides of ribbing in place.

FINISHING

Sew sleeves in place under armhole trim, centering sleeve on shoulder seam. Sew sleeve seams. Sew side seams, leaving seams open for pockets. Cut two 5"/12.5cm squares of fabric for breast pocket and four 7"/17.5cm squares for side pockets. With right sides facing and allowing 1/2"/1cm for seam, sew 2 matching pieces tog along 3 sides. Sew pocket linings in place and turn in to wrong side.

CLOCHE

SIZES

Directions are for small, with medium and large in parentheses. Finished measurements 21¼ (22½,23¾)"/53 (56.5,60) cm in diameter.

MATERIALS

1¾ (1¾,3½) oz/50 (50,100) gr bulky boucle yarn (MC), 1oz/30gr bulky weight yarn (CC)

NEEDLES

One pair size 10/6mm knitting needles

GAUGE

4 sts = 1"/2.5cm and 9 rows = 2"/5cm on size 10 needles over st st

With CC, cast on 85 (90,95) sts. Work in st st for 2½"/6cm. Change to MC and continue in reverse st st until 7½ (8½,9½)"/19 (21.5,24) cm from beg. End with p side facing.

SHAPE CROWN

1st dec row: *K 3, k 2 tog; repeat from * across. P 1 row. 2nd dec row: *K 2, k 2 tog; repeat from * across. P 1 row. 3rd dec row: *K 1, k 2 tog; repeat from * across. P 1 row. 4th dec row: K 2 tog across. Last row: K 2 tog across; end with k 1 (0,1). Cut yarn, leaving a 15"/38cm end. Thread yarn through rem sts. Fasten off securely. Sew back seam, taking care to sew seam on cuff so that it is on right side of cuff (wrong side of hat).

SILK BLEND TUNICS

THESE SWEATERS ARE AN EXCELLENT EXAMPLE OF HOW ONE PATTERN CAN LOOK
COMPLETELY DIFFERENT WHEN YOU USE A DIFFERENT YARN AND REVERSE THE RIGHT SIDE
OF THE GARMENT. NOTE THAT THE TYPE OF YARN USED AFFECTS THE AMOUNT NEEDED.

SIZES

Directions are for girl's small, with medium and large
in parentheses. Finished chest measurements 35
(37,40)"/89 (94,101.5) cm; length to back neck edge
26 (28,30)"/66 (71,76) cm; armhole measures 16
(18,20)"/40.5 (45.5,51) cm; length of sleeve from
underarm 17 (18,19)"/43 (45.5,48.5) cm.

MATERIALS

For sweater pictured on right: 21½
(25,28½) oz/600 (700,800) gr worsted
weight silk/wool blend 116 (128,140) 1/4"
beads, matching sewing thread
For sweater pictured on left: 12¼ (14,15¾) oz/350
(400,450) gr silk/mohair blend

NEEDLES

One each 24"/61cm size 6/4mm and size 8/5mm
circular knitting needles, or size needed to obtain
gauge
1 set each size 6/4mm and size 8/5mm double-
pointed needles
6 stitch holders

GAUGE

4 sts and 5 rows = 1"/2.5cm on size 8 needles over st st

Note: Both sweaters are made in the same manner, but the tunic on the right is assembled with the p side as the right side and has beads knitted into the collar and sleeves. The tunic on the left is assembled with the k side as the right side.

BODY

With smaller circular needle and MC, cast on 140 (148,160) sts. Taking care not to twist st, join and work around in k 1, p 1 ribbing for 1"/2.5cm. Mark beg of rnd; carry marker. Change to larger needle and work in st st (k every row) until piece measures 18 (19,20)"/45.5 (48,51) cm from beg.

DIVIDE FOR FRONT AND BACK

Bind off 2 sts, work next 68 (72,78) sts and sl to holder for front, bind off 2 sts, k to end. Working back and forth in st st (k 1 row, p 1 row), work even until 8 (9,10)"/20 (23,25) cm above dividing row. Sl 23 (24,26) sts to holder for right shoulder, 22 (24,26) sts to holder for collar, and rem 23 (24,26) sts to holder for left shoulder.

FRONT

Sl sts from holder to needle and work as for back until 5 (6,7)"/12.5 (15,18) cm above dividing row. Mark center 18 (20,22) sts.

SHAPE NECK

Work to first marker; with new strand, work to next marker and sl sts between markers to holder for collar; work to end. Working both sides simultaneously, dec 1 st at each neck edge every other row until 23 (24,26) sts rem for each shoulder. Work even until same length as back to shoulders. Sl sts to holders.

SLEEVES

With smaller dp needles, cast on 32 (36,40) sts and divide on 3 needles. Taking care not to twist, work in k 1, p 1 ribbing for 3"/7.5cm. Mark beg of row; carry marker. Change to larger dp needles and st st, and inc 1 st in each st on first row—64 (72,80) sts.

FOR BEADED SLEEVE

Work 3 rnds even. Thread 32 (36,40) beads directly onto yarn and attach at beg of rnd. 1st beading rnd: *K 7, k 1 with bead; repeat from * around. K 3 rnds. 2nd beading row: K 3, *k 1 with bead, k 7; repeat from * around, end k 5. K 3 rnds. Repeat last 8 rnds once. Push beads to p side of work.

FOR BOTH SLEEVES

Work even in st st until 17 (18,19)"/43 (45.5,48) cm from beg. Bind off.

FINISHING

Block lightly. With p side as right side for sweater at right and k side as right side for sweater at left, weave shoulder seams; sew in sleeves, easing to fit.

COWL COLLAR

With wrong side facing and smaller dp needles, k across sts from back neck holder, pick up and k 19 sts to front neck holder, k across sts of front holder, pick up and k 19 sts to shoulder—78 (82,86) sts. Work around in reverse st st or st st to match body for 3"/7.5cm, inc 0 (2,4) sts across back neck on first rnd. 1st inc rnd: *Work 5, inc in next st; repeat from * Work even until 6"/15cm from beg. 2nd inc rnd: *Work 6, inc in next st; repeat from * around.

FOR BEADED COWL COLLAR

Thread 52 (56,60) beads onto yarn and join at beg of rnd. 1st beading rnd: *P 7, p 1 with bead; repeat from * around. P 3 rnds. 2nd beading rnd: P 3, *p 1 with bead, p 7; repeat from * around; end p 5. Push beads to p side of work.

FOR BOTH COWL COLLARS

Work even until 8"/20cm from beg. Work 3 rows of k 1, p 1 ribbing. Bind off loosely in ribbing.

BALLERINA VEST AND LEGWARMERS

PERFECT WARM-UP WEAR—CHOOSE A HOT COLOR FOR JAZZ CLASS OR PALE PINK FOR BALLET.

VEST

SIZES
Directions are for girl's small, with medium and large in parentheses. Finished chest measurements 34½ (37½,40)"/88 (95,102) cm; length from waist to back neck edge 22½ (24,26)"/57 (61,66) cm.

MATERIALS
8¾ (10½,12¼) oz/250 (300,350) gr sportweight brushed mohair blend yarn
2 yd/1.8m length matching or contrasting satin ribbon, 7/8"/2cm wide

NEEDLES
One pair size 6/4mm needles, or size needed to obtain gauge
Crochet hook size D/3.25mm

GAUGE
11 sts and 13 rows = 2"/5cm on size 6 needles over st st

BACK
Cast on 95 (103,111) sts. Work in st st for 1"/2.5cm for hem; end with p row. Eyelet turning row: *K 2 tog, yo; repeat from * across; end with k 1. P next row, working p in yo of eyelet row. Continue in st st until 4"/10cm above eyelet row. End with right side facing. Ribbon casing: *K 1, wrap yarn around needle 4 times; repeat from * across; end with k 1. Next row: P across, dropping all yo off needle. Continue in st st until 11½ (12,13)"/29.5 (31,33.5) cm from casing row. End with right side facing.

SHAPE ARMHOLES
Bind off 6 sts at beg of next 2 rows. Dec 1 st at each edge every other row 4 times. Work even in st st until armhole measures 7 (8,9)"/18 (20,23) cm. End with right side facing.

SHAPE SHOULDERS
Bind off 8 (9,10) sts at beg of next 6 rows. Bind off remaining sts.

FRONT
Work same as back until armhole measures 1"/2.5cm. End with right side facing.

SHAPE V-NECK

Mark center st. K to marked st; with 2nd strand, bind off center st, k to end. Working both sides simultaneously, dec 1 st at each neck edge every other row 13 (14,15) times. Work even on rem 24 (27,30) sts until same length as back to shoulders. Bind off from each armhole edge 8 (9,10) sts 3 times.

FINISHING

Sew left shoulder seam. With right side facing, and D hook, and taking care to keep work flat, sc into every other bound-off st across back neck, sc into every other row down front neck edge, sc in center st, sc up neck edge to shoulder; ch 1, turn; *sc in next st, ch 1, sl st in same st; repeat from * around. Fasten off. Sew right shoulder and neckband seam. Armhole edging: With right side facing, and D hook, sc in every other bound-off st and row around armhole edge. Complete edging as for neckband. Sew side seams. Turn hem to wrong side along eyelet row and sew in place. Beg at center front, weave ribbon through ribbon casing.

LEGWARMERS

SIZE

One size fits all.

MATERIALS

5¼oz/150gr sportweight mohair blend yarn
3/4"/7.5cm width elastic to fit around thighs at top of legwarmers

NEEDLES

One pair size 6/4mm needles, or size needed to obtain gauge

GAUGE

11 sts and 13 rows = 2"/5cm in st st

(Make Two):

Beg at bottom edge with stirrup, cast on 67 sts. Work in k 1, p 1 ribbing for 8 rows. Working in ribbing, bind off 16 sts at beg of next 2 rows—35 sts. Change to st st, and inc 1 st each edge on next row, then every other row 3 times more—43 sts. Cast on 6 sts at end of next 2 rows—55 sts. Continue in st st, inc 1 st each edge every 1"/2.5cm until 23"/56cm from beg or desired length. End with right side facing. Eyelet row: *K 2 tog, yo; repeat from * across; end k 1. Continue in st st for 1"/2.5cm for hem. Bind off loosely.

FINISHING

Sew back seam. Sew stirrup seam. Turn hem under on eyelet row and sew in place, leaving an opening for elastic. Insert elastic; adjust length to fit; sew ends. Sew hem closed.

Icelandic Pullover

A RUGGED, OUTDOOR PULLOVER WITH ALL THE EASE
OF A SWEATSHIRT BUT SO MUCH MORE STYLE. DEER HORN
BUTTONS COMPLETE THE WILD AND WOOLLY LOOK.

SIZES

Directions are for boy's small, with medium and
large in parentheses. Finished chest measurements
36 (38,42)"/91.5 (97,106.5) cm; length to back neck
edge 24 (26,28)"/61 (66,71) cm; armhole measures
16 (18,20)"/40.5 (45.5,50.5) cm; length of sleeve
from underarm 18 (19,20)"/45.5 (48,51) cm.

MATERIALS

15¾ (17½,19¼) oz/450 (500,550) gr Icelandic
boucle wool in MC, and 1¾ (3½,3½) oz/50
(100,100) gr lightweight Icelandic wool in
CC Three 7-8"/2cm deer horn buttons

NEEDLES

One pair size 6/4mm and two pairs size
8/5mm needles, or size needed to obtain
gauge 5 stitch holders

GAUGE

4 sts and 5 rows = 1"/2.5cm on size 8
needles over st st

BACK

With smaller needles and CC, cast on 71 (75,83)
sts. Work in k 1, p 1 ribbing for 2¼"/5.5cm. Inc 1 st at
end of last row. Change to larger needles and MC,
and work in reverse st st until 16 (17,18)"/40.5
(43,45.5) cm from beg. End with right side facing.

SHAPE ARMHOLES

Bind off 4 sts at beg of next 2 rows. Continue in reverse st st until armhole measures 8 (9,10)"/15
(18,25.5) cm. Sl 22 (24,26) sts to holder for shoulder, 20 (20,24) sts to holder for neckband, and rem
sts to holder for other shoulder.

FRONT

Work same as for back until 3"/7.5cm from beg. End with right side facing. Divide for pocket: In reverse st st, work 16 sts, sl next 40 (44,52) sts to holder and hold to front, cast on 40 (44,52) sts, work 16 sts to end. Work even in reverse st st until 9"/23cm from beg. Sl sts to holder. Sl sts for pocket to needle and work in reverse st st until 9"/23cm from beg. End right side facing. Join pocket and lining: Sl sts from holder to spare needle. Keeping to reverse st st, work 16 sts from spare needle, holding pocket sts against lining, *p 1 st from pocket tog with 1 st from lining; repeat from * across until only 16 sts rem on back needle; p to end. Continue to work as for back until armhole measures 1 (2,3)"/2.5 (5,7.5) cm. End with right side facing.

SHAPE PLACKET

Mark center 4 sts. Work to first marker; with new strand of MC, bind off 4 sts; work to end. Working both sides simultaneously, work even until armhole measures 5 (6,7)"/12 (15,18) cm. End with right side facing.

SHAPE NECK

Bind off 4 sts at each neck edge on next 2 rows, then dec 1 st each edge every other row 4 (4,6) times. Work even on rem 22 (24,26) sts until same length as back to shoulder. Sl sts to holders.

SLEEVES

With smaller needles and CC, cast on 35 (37,39) sts. Work in k 1, p 1 ribbing for 2"/5cm. Inc 1 st at end of last row. Change to larger needles and MC. Working in reverse st st, inc 1 st each edge every 4th row 14 (17,20) times—64 (72,80) sts. Work even until 18 (19,20)"/45.5 (48,51) sts from beg. Bind off.

FINISHING

Block pieces lightly. Pocket edgings: Right side facing, with smaller needles and CC, pick up and k 1 st at beg of pocket, 45 st along edge of pocket, and 1 st at end. Work in k 1, p 1 ribbing for 1"/2.5cm. Bind off loosely in ribbing. Work other side to correspond. Right placket edging: Right side facing, with smaller needles and CC, beg 2 rows below edge of placket, pick up and k 27 sts along edge. Work in k 1, p 1 ribbing for 1"/2.5cm. Bind off. Left placket edging: Mark edge for 3 buttonholes, evenly spaced, with the first buttonhole 1 st from neck edge and the last ½"/1cm from bottom edge. Work as for right edging, working buttonholes opposite markers on 3rd row as follows: Work 1 st, *bind off 2 sts, work to next marker; repeat from * twice; end at bottom edge. On next row, cast on 2 sts over bound-off sts. Join shoulder seams. Neckband: With smaller needles and CC, right side facing, beg at front edge of placket edging, pick up and k 29 (29,31) sts to shoulder, k across 20 (20,24) sts from back holder, pick up and k 29 (29,31) sts to front edge of placket. Work in k 1, p 1 ribbing for 1"/2.5cm. Bind off. Sew in sleeves, centering sleeves on shoulder seams. Sew side and sleeve seams. Tack pocket ribbings in place. Sew pocket lining in place. Sew on buttons.

GIRL'S ICELANDIC OUTERWEAR

A WOOL FLANNEL LINING WILL KEEP THE COLD WINDS FROM BLOWING
THROUGH THIS HEAVY WOOL VEST. MATCHING ACCESSORIES ARE EDGED
WITH A NUBBLY WOOL BOUCLE.

VEST

SIZES

Directions are for girl's small, with medium and large
in parentheses. Finished chest measurements 36
(38,40)"/91.5 (96.5,101.5) cm; length to back neck
edge 22 (24,26)"/56 (61,66) cm.

MATERIALS

13 (14,16) oz/370 (400,455) gr bulky weight yarn in
snow (MC), and 4oz/115gr each mulberry (A), winesap (B), and elderberry (C)
¾yd/.7m of 45"/115cm wide flannel fabric for
lining (optional)
7 (7,8) 3/4" pewter buttons

NEEDLES

One pair each size 8/5mm and size 10/6mm
needles, or size needed to obtain gauge
One each size G/4mm and H/5mm crochet hooks
7 stitch holders

GAUGE

4 sts = 1"/2.5cm and 9 rows = 2"/5cm on size 10
needles over st st

BACK

With smaller needles and A, cast on 71 (75,79) sts.
Work in k 1, p 1 ribbing for 2"/5cm. Inc 1 st at end of
last row. Change to larger needles and st st, and
work pattern following chart I. Continue in st st with
MC until 14 (15,16)"/35.5 (38,40.5) cm from beg.
End with right side facing.

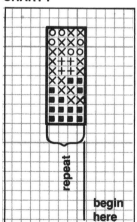

CHART I

KEY:

- ◯ = MC (snow)
- ■ = A (mulberry)
- ⊠ = B (winesap)
- ⊞ = C (elderberry)

repeat

begin
here

SHAPE ARMHOLES

Bind off 4 sts at beg of next 2 rows, then dec 1 st each edge every other row 4 times. Continue in st st and work pattern from chart II. Work 2 rows even with MC, then work pattern from chart I. Work even in A until armhole measures 8 (9,10)"/20 (23,25.5) cm. Sl 16 (18,20) sts to holder for shoulder, 24 sts to holder for neckband, and rem sts to holder for other shoulder.

CHART II

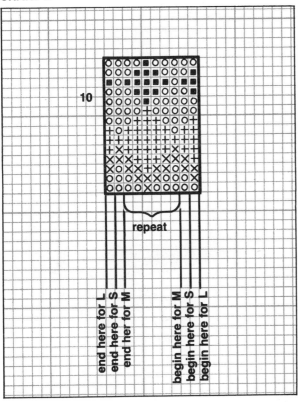

RIGHT FRONT

With smaller needles and A, cast on 35 (37,39) sts. Work in k 1, p 1 ribbing for 2"/5cm. Inc 1 st at end of last row. Change to larger needles and st st.

DIVIDE FOR POCKET

Following chart III, work 24 sts; sl remaining sts to holder for front. Keeping to st st and pattern following chart III, work even on 24 sts to end of chart, then continue in MC until pocket measures 7"/18cm from beg of chart III pattern. Sl sts to holder. Sl sts for front to left needle; with MC, cast on 24 sts on same needle. Work in st st, with MC on first 24 sts and chart III on last 12 (14,16) sts. When chart III is completed, work even in MC until 7"/18cm above beg of chart III. End with right side facing.

CHART III

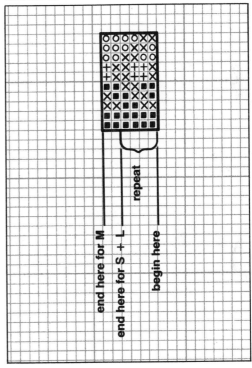

JOIN POCKET AND LINING

Sl pocket sts to extra needle, hold against lining sts, *k 1 st from pocket tog with st from lining; repeat from * across until all pocket sts are worked, k across rem sts. Continue to work even in st st and MC until 14 (15,16)"/35.5 (38,40.5) cm from beg. End with wrong side facing.

SHAPE ARMHOLE

Bind off 4 sts at beg of next row, then dec 1 st at armhole edge on next row, then every other row 3 times more. End right side facing. Continue in st st, following chart IV. When chart IV is complete, work 2 rows st st in MC. Work chart II until armhole measures 5 (6,7)"/12.5 (15,18) cm. End with right side facing.

CHART V

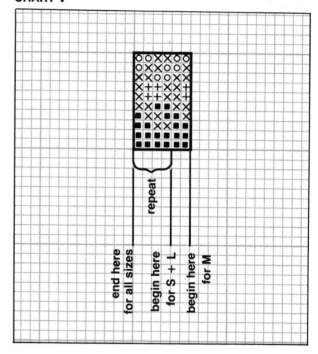

CHART IV

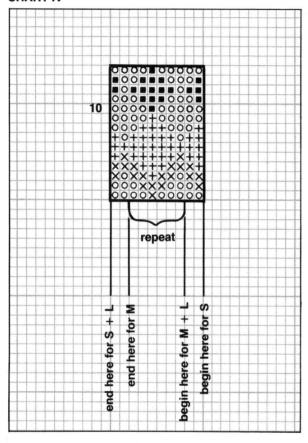

CHART VI

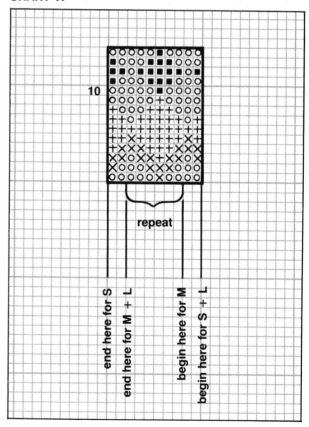

SHAPE NECK

Work first 10 sts and sl to holder for front neck, then dec 1 st from neck edge every other row 2 times. Work even, continuing with A when chart II is completed, until same length as back to shoulder. Sl sts to holder for shoulder.

LEFT FRONT

Work as for right front, reversing shaping and substituting chart V for chart III and chart VI for chart IV.

FINISHING

Block pieces lightly. Using knitted pieces as pattern, cut lining, allowing ⅝"/1cm seam allowance and ending lining at top of ribbing after edge is turned under. Sew lining shoulder and side seams. Press seams. Join vest shoulder seams. Neckband: With right side facing, smaller needles, and MC, k across sts from right front holder, pick up and k 17 sts to shoulder, k across sts from back neck holder, pick up and k 17 sts to front neck holder, k sts from front holder. Work in k 1, p 1 ribbing from 1"/2.5cm. Bind off loosely in ribbing.

ARMHOLE EDGINGS

With H hook, MC, and right side facing, sc in end of every other row along armhole edge. Ch 1, turn; sc in each sc. Fasten off MC. With B, work 1 more row sc. Fasten off.

LEFT FRONT EDGING

With H hook, MC, and right side facing, sc in every other st along edge, working pocket and pocket lining tog; ch 1, turn, sc in each sc. Fasten off.

RIGHT FRONT EDGING

Mark for 7 (7,8) buttonholes evenly spaced along front edge. Work edging as for left front, working buttonholes at markers on 2nd row as follows: *Work to 1 st before marker, ch 2, sk 2 sts, sc in next st; repeat from *; sc to end.

FRONT TRIMMING ROW

With H hook and right side facing, join B at bottom edge, sc in each sc to neck edge, change to G hook, sc in same st as last sc, sc in each st of ribbing, change to H hook, sc in same st as last st, sc in each sc to end. Fasten off.

POCKET EDGINGS

With size H hook, B, and right side facing, work 1 row sc along pocket edge.

Sew side and armband seams. Sew pocket linings in place. Sew buttons opposite buttonholes. Pin lining in place; turn raw edges in and sew in place, easing to fit.

SOCKS

SIZE
One size fits all.

MATERIALS
8oz/230gr bulky yarn in elderberry (MC), 3oz/85gr winesap (A), 1oz/30gr mulberry (B), and 4oz/115gr bulky wool boucle in natural (C)

NEEDLES
One set each size 8/5mm and 10/6mm double-pointed needles, or size needed to obtain gauge

GAUGE
4 sts = 1"/2.5cm and 9 rows = 2"/5cm on size 10 needles over st st

(MAKE TWO)
With smaller needles and C, cast on 54 sts, evenly divided on 3 needles. Taking care not to twist sts, join. P around for 2½/6.25cm. For drawstring opening, p 26, bind off next 2 sts, p 26, p next rnd, casting 2 sts over bound-off sts. Continue to p until cuff measures 5"/12.5cm. Change to larger needles and MC and work in st st (k every rnd) for 4 rnds, dec 2 sts evenly spaced on last rnd. Continue in st st, following chart I for pattern. When chart I is completed, k 3 rnds MC. 1st dec rnd: With MC, *k 11, k 2 tog; repeat from * around. Work pattern from chart II, then k 3 rnds MC. 2nd dec rnd: With MC, *k 10, k 2 tog; repeat from * around. Work pattern from chart I, then work 3 rnds MC. 3rd dec rnd: With MC, *k 9, k 2 tog; repeat from * around. Work pattern from chart II. Work 1 rnd MC, dec 2 sts evenly spaced on rnd. Work even in MC until 11¾"/30cm from beg, or desired length to ankle.

CHART I

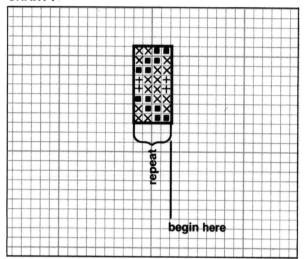

repeat

begin here

KEY:

■ = MC (elderberry)

☒ = A (winesap)

⊞ = B (mulberry)

NOTE: Colors in key are different from vest and hat and mittens.

CHART II

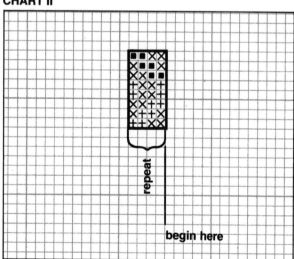

repeat

begin here

SHAPE HEEL

Divide sts so that 19 sts are on 1 needle for heel, and 19 sts are divided between 2 needles for instep. Work to heel sts, then work back and forth on heel sts as follows: K 1, *sl 1, k 1; repeat from * across. P 1 row. Repeat these rows until there are 7 sl st rows, ending with a sl st row.

TURN HEEL

P 11, p 2 tog, p 1; turn. Short rows: Row 1: Sl 1 as to k, k 4, k 2 tog, k 1; turn. Row 2: Sl 1 as if to p, p 5, p 2 tog, p 1; turn. Continue as for rows 1 and 2, having 1 more st between decreases in each row, until there are 11 sts (this will be a k row). Pick up and k 7 sts along side edge of heel, k across 19 sts of instep, pick up and k 7 sts along other side of heel, k across 6 sts of bottom of heel. Divide sts on needles as follows: 1st needle—5 sts from bottom of heel and 7 sts from side edge; 2nd needle—19 sts from instep; 3rd needle—7 sts from side edge and 6 sts from bottom of heel. Decrease as follows: Rnd 1: Work to 3 sts before end of first needle, k 2 tog, k 1; k across 2nd needle; on 3rd needle, k 1, k 2 tog. K 1 rnd. Repeat these 2 rnds until there are a total of 19 sts on first and third needles combined. Work even in st st until 6½"/15.5cm from back of heel, or about 2½"/6cm from desired length.

SHAPE TOE

Rnd 1: K until 2 sts from end of 1st needle, k 2 tog; on 2nd needle, k 1, sl 1, k 1, psso, k across until 3 sts from end, k 2 tog, k 1; on 3rd needle, k 2 tog, k to end. K 1 rnd. Repeat these 2 rnds until 14 sts rem. Sl sts from 3rd needle to first needle. Holding 2 needles tog, weave sts of toe.

FINISHING

Steam lightly. Turn cuff in half to inside and sew in place. To make ties for cuffs, use 6 strands of yarn and braid lengths of 28" or desired length. Thread braids through bound-off sts in cuff.

HAT

SIZES

Directions are for small with medium and large in parentheses. Finished measurements 21 (22½,24)"/53.5 (57,61) cm in diameter.

MATERIALS

3oz/85gr bulky yarn in snow (MC), and ½oz/15gr each mulberry (A), winesap (B), elderberry (C), and 3oz/85gr bulky wool boucle in mulberry (D)

NEEDLES

One pair size 10/6mm knitting needles, or size needed to obtain gauge
One set size 8/5mm double-pointed needles

GAUGE

4 sts = 1"/2.5cm and 9 rows = 2"/5cm on size 10 needles over st st

Note: Brim is worked as a tube that goes around head; crown is worked along side of tube.

BRIM

With D and size 8 needles, cast on 24 sts evenly divided on 3 needles. Taking care not to twist sts, join and work around in st st until 21 (22½,24)"/53.5 (57,61) cm. Bind off. Turn tube so p side is out.

CROWN

With MC and larger needles, pick up and k 84 (90,96) sts along edge of brim. P 1 row MC. Continue in st st, following chart I. P 1 row MC.

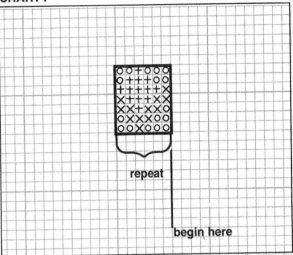

CHART I

KEY:

☐ = MC (snow)

■ = A (mulberry)

☒ = B (winesap)

⊞ = C (elderberry)

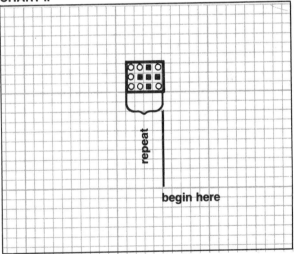

CHART II

SHAPE TOP

1st dec row: *K 4, k 2 tog; repeat from * across. P 1 row. 2nd dec row: *K 3, k 2 tog; repeat from * across. P 1 row. Work chart II in st st. Continuing in MC, p 1 row. 3rd dec row: *K 2, k 2 tog; repeat from * across. P 1 row. 4th dec row: *K 1, k 2 tog; repeat from * across. Fasten off MC. 5th dec row: With B, k 2 tog across. P 1 row. Fasten off B. 6th dec row: With C, k 2 tog across; end k 0 (1,0). P 1 row. Fasten off C. 7th dec row: With A, k 2 tog across; end k 1 (0,0). P 1 row. Cut yarn, leaving a 15"/38cm end. Thread yarn through rem sts. Fasten off securely. Sew back seam, weaving ends of brim (tube) tog.

MITTENS

SIZES
One size fits all.

MATERIALS
4oz/115gr bulky yarn in mulberry (MC), ½oz/15gr each winesap (A) and elderberry (B), and 1oz/30gr bulky wool boucle in mulberry (C)

NEEDLES
One set each size 8/5mm and size 10/6mm double-pointed needles, or size needed to obtain gauge 1 stitch holder

GAUGE
4 sts = 1"/2.5cm and 9 rows = 2"/5cm on size 10 needles over st st

LEFT MITTEN
With smaller needles and C, cast on 36 sts evenly divided on 3 needles. Taking care not to twist sts, join. P around for 1"/2.5cm for cuff. Change to larger needles and MC and work in st st (k every rnd) for 3 rnds. Continue in st st, following chart I for pattern. When chart I is completed, k 3 rnds MC. Change to size 8 needles and work in k 1, p 1 ribbing for 1"/2.5cm. Change back to size 10 needles. K 3 rnds.

CHART I

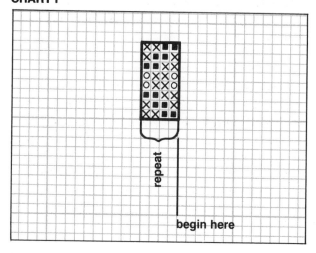

begin here

KEY:

■ = MC (mulberry)

☒ = A (winesap)

☐ = B (elderberry)

NOTE: Colors in key are different from vest and hat and socks.

START THUMB
Work 2 sts, place marker to beg thumb, *inc 1 in next st; repeat from * once, place marker to end thumb, work to end. Working in st st, inc 1 st each edge of thumb inside markers every other row until there are 10 sts between markers. Next rnd: K to first marker, sl 10 sts between markers to holder to be worked later for thumb, cast on 2 sts, k to end of

CHART II

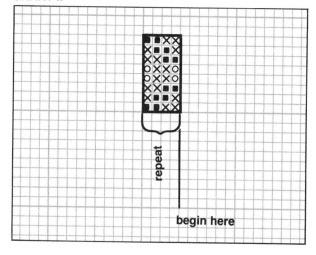

begin here

rnd—36 sts. Work even in st st and MC until 7½"/19cm above cuff or 2"/5cm less than desired length of mitten.

SHAPE TOP

1st dec rnd: *K 4, k 2 tog; repeat from * around. K 1 rnd. 2nd dec rnd: *K 3, k 2 tog; repeat from * around. K 1 rnd. 3rd dec rnd: *K 2, k 2 tog; repeat from * around. K 1 rnd. 4th dec rnd: *K 1, k 2 tog; repeat from * around. 5th dec rnd: *K 2 tog; repeat from * around. K 1 rnd. Cut yarn, leaving a 12"/30.5cm end. Thread end through rem sts and fasten off securely.

FINISH THUMB

Sl 10 sts from holder to 2 needles, pick up and k 8 sts along thumbhole edge. Work even in st st for 1"/2.5cm. Work dec as for top for 8 rows. Cut yarn and fasten off as for top.

RIGHT MITTEN

Work as for left mitten, following chart II for pattern.

FINISHING

Block lightly. Turn boucle edging in half to wrong side and tack in place.

BOY'S ICELANDIC VEST AND HAT

NATURAL SHEEP COLORS COMBINE IN THIS ICELANDIC-STYLE VEST. THE DEEP POCKETS
AND ZIPPER CLOSURE WILL MAKE IT A FAVORITE WITH YOUNG
OUTDOORSMEN. ADD THE HAT, AND THIS SET WILL WEAR LONG INTO WINTER.

VEST

SIZES
Directions are for boy's small, with medium and
large in parentheses. Finished chest measurements
36 (39,42)"/91.5 (99,106.5) cm; length to back neck
edge 22 (24,26)"/56 (61,66) cm.

MATERIALS
14 (16,18) oz/400 (455,510) gr bulky weight yarn in
loam (MC), 4oz/115gr each bark (A) and mist (B)
One 18 (20,22)"/45.5 (51,56) cm separating zipper
¾yd/.7m of 45"/115cm wide flannel fabric for lining
(optional)

NEEDLES
One pair each size 8/5mm and size 10/6mm
needles, or size needed to obtain gauge
7 stitch holders

GAUGE
4 sts = 1"/2.5cm and 9 rows = 2"/5cm on size 10
needles over st st

BACK
With smaller needles and MC, cast on 71 (77,83)
sts. Work in k 1, p 1 ribbing for 2¼"/5.5cm. Inc 1 st at
end of last row. Change to larger needles and st st,
and work in pattern following chart I, then continue
in st st with MC until 14 (15,16)"/35.5 (38,40.5) cm
from beg. End with right side facing.

CHART I

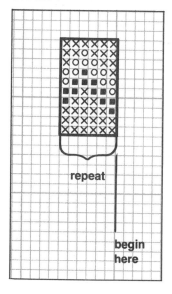

repeat

begin
here

KEY:

☒ = MC (loam)

■ = A (bark)

◯ = B (mist)

SHAPE ARMHOLES

Bind off 4 sts at beg of next 2 rows, then dec 1 st each edge every other row 4 times. Continue in st st and work pattern from chart II, then work even in MC until armhole measures 8 (9,10)"/20.5 (23,25.5) cm. Sl 18 (20,23) sts to holder for shoulder, 20 (22,22) sts to holder for neckband, and rem sts to holder for other shoulder.

CHART II

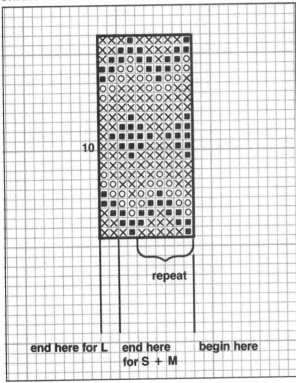

10

repeat

end here for L | **end here for S + M** | **begin here**

RIGHT FRONT

With smaller needles and MC, cast on 38 (42,44) sts. Row 1: K 2, *k 1, p 1; repeat from * across. Row 2: *P 1, k 1; repeat from * until 2 sts rem; k 2. Repeat these 2 rows until 2¼"/5.5cm from beg. End with right side facing. Change to larger needles.

DIVIDE FOR POCKET

With MC, k 2 (edge sts). Following chart III, work 24 sts; cast on 2 st in MC for edge sts; sl remaining sts to holder for front. Keeping edge sts in garter st and

MC, work 24 sts in st st and pattern following chart III, work even on 28 sts to end of chart, then continue in MC until pocket measures 7"/18cm from beg of chart III pattern. Sl sts to holder. Sl sts for front to left needle; with MC, cast on 24 sts on same needle. Work in st st, with MC on first 24 sts and chart III on last 12 (16,18) sts. When chart III is completed, work even in MC until 7"/18cm above beg of chart III. End with right side facing.

CHART III

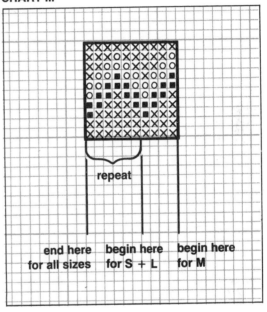

repeat

end here for all sizes | **begin here for S + L** | **begin here for M**

JOIN POCKET AND LINING

Sl pocket sts to extra needle, hold against lining sts, k 2 sts from pocket, *k 1 st from pocket tog with st from lining; repeat from * across until all pocket sts are worked; k across rem sts. Continue to work even in st st and MC, keeping 2 sts at front edge in garter st, until 14 (15,16)"/35.5 (38,40.5) cm from beg. End with wrong side facing.

SHAPE ARMHOLE

Bind off 4 sts at beg of next row, then dec 1 st at armhole edge on next row, then every other row 3 times more. End right side facing. Continue in st st, following chart IV, with edge sts in MC and garter st. At same time, when armhole measures 5 (6,7)"/12.5 (15,18) cm, end with right side facing.

CHART IV

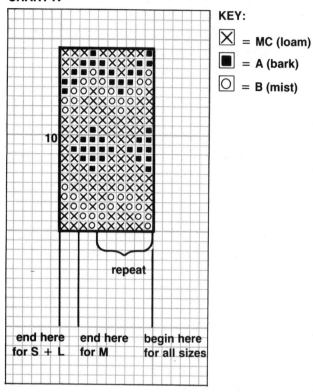

KEY:

☒ = MC (loam)

■ = A (bark)

⊡ = B (mist)

10

repeat

end here
for S + L

end here
for M

begin here
for all sizes

SHAPE NECK

Work first 8 (10,10) sts and sl to holder for front neck, then dec 1 st from neck edge every other row 4 (4,3) times. Work even, continuing with MC when chart is completed, until same length as back to shoulder. Sl sts to holder for shoulder.

LEFT FRONT

Cast on as for right front. Row 1: K 1, p 1; repeat from * until 2 sts rem; k 2. Row 2: K 2, *k 1, p 1; repeat from * to end. Repeat these 2 rows until 2¼"/5.5cm from beg. End with right side facing. Change to larger needles and st st.

DIVIDE FOR POCKET

Work across 12 (16,18) sts following chart V; still following chart, cast on 2 sts; cast on 24 more sts with MC for pocket lining. Sl rem 26 sts to holder for pocket. Work even in st st, with patterns as established, until 7"/18cm from beg of chart V. Sl sts to holder. Cast on 2 sts with MC, sl 26 pocket sts to needle and work as for right front, following chart V until 7"/18cm from beg of chart V.

CHART V

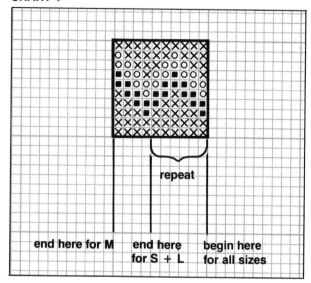

repeat

end here for M

end here
for S + L

begin here
for all sizes

JOIN POCKET AND LINING

Sl sts from front and pocket lining to spare needle. Beg at side edge, p 10 (14,16) sts, *p 1 st from pocket tog with st from lining; repeat from * across until all lining sts are worked; k 2 edge sts. Continue as for right front, reversing shaping, and following chart VI for pattern.

CHART VI

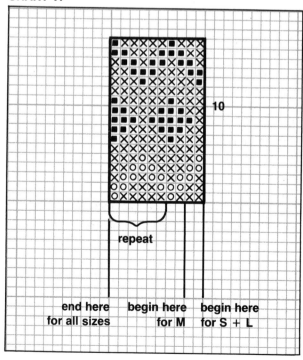

10

repeat

end here
for all sizes

begin here
for M

begin here
for S + L

FINISHING

Block pieces lightly. Using knitted pieces as pattern, cut lining, allowing ⅝"/1cm seam allowance, and ending lining at top of ribbing after edge is turned under. Sew lining shoulder and side seams. Press seams. Join vest shoulder seams. Neckband: With right side facing, smaller needles, and MC, k across sts from right front holder, pick up and k 15 sts to shoulder, k across sts from back neck holder, pick up and k 15 sts to front neck holder, k sts from front holder. Keeping 2 sts at each front edge in garter st, work in k 1, p 1 ribbing for 1"/2.5cm. Bind off loosely in ribbing.

ARMHOLE EDGINGS

With smaller needles and MC, right side facing, pick up and k 73 (81,91) sts along armhole edge. Work in k 1, p 1 ribbing for 1"/2.5cm. Bind off loosely in ribbing. Sew side and armband seams. Sew pocket edges in place. Sew pocket linings to ribbing and front edge. Sew zipper along front edges. Pin lining in place; turn raw edges in and sew in place, easing to fit.

HAT

SIZES

Directions are for small, with medium and large in parentheses. Finished measurements 21 (22½,24)"/53.5 (57,61) cm.

MATERIALS

4oz/115gr bulky yarn in loam (MC), and 1oz/30gr each bark (A) and mist (B)

NEEDLES

One pair each size 8/5mm and 10/6mm knitting needles, or size needed to obtain gauge

GAUGE

4 sts = 1"/2.5cm and 9 rows = 2"/5cm with size 10 needles over st st

With smaller needles and CC, cast on 83 (89,95) sts. Work in k 1, p 1 ribbing for 2½"/6cm. K 1 row for turning ridge. Continue in ribbing until 5"/12.5cm from beg. Inc 1 st at end of last row. Change to larger needles and MC, and continue in st st, following chart. P 1 row.

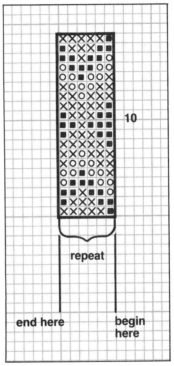

KEY:

⊠ = MC (loam)

■ = A (bark)

▣ = B (mist)

10

repeat

end here   begin here

SHAPE CROWN

1st dec row: *K 4, k 2 tog; repeat from * across. P 1 row. 2nd dec row: *K 3, k 2 tog; repeat from * across. P 1 row. 3rd dec row: *K 2, k 2 tog; repeat from * across. P 1 row. 4th dec row: *K 1, k 2 tog; repeat from * across. P 1 row. 5th dec row: K 2 tog across. P 1 row. 6th dec row: K 2 tog across; end k 0 (1,0). 7th dec row: P 2 tog across; end p 1 (0,0). Cut yarn, leaving a 15"/38cm end. Thread yarn through rem sts. Fasten off securely. Sew back seam, taking care to sew seam on cuff so that it is on right side of cuff (wrong side of hat).

FEMININE FAIR ISLE SWEATER SET

A TRADITIONAL FAIR ISLE PATTERN TRIMS THE EDGES
OF THIS SWEATER SET, KNITTED IN A VERY FINE SHETLAND
WOOL IN DISTINCTIVE, UNTRADITIONAL COLORS.

CARDIGAN

SIZES
Directions are for girl's small, with medium and large in parentheses. Finished chest measurements (buttoned) 36 (38½,41)"/92 (98.5,105) cm; length to back neck edge 20 (22,23)"/51 (56,58.5) cm; armhole measures 12½ (13½,14)"/32 (35,36.5)cm; length of sleeve from underarm 15½ (16½,17½)"/39.5 (42,45) cm.

MATERIALS
10 (12,14) oz/340 (400,475) gr Shetland wool in aubergine (MC), and 1oz/30gr each plum (A), teal (B), and magenta (C)
8 (8,9) ½" buttons

NEEDLES
One each size 2/2.75mm and size 4/3.5mm circular needles, or size needed to obtain gauge
One set each size 2/2.75mm and 4/3.5mm double-pointed knitting needles
3 stitch holders

GAUGE
13 sts = 2"/5cm and 8 rows = 1"/2.5cm on size 4 needles over st st

BODY
With smaller circular needle and MC, cast on 243 (259,275) sts. Working back and forth, work in k 1, p 1 ribbing for 1¼"/4cm. With right side facing, work buttonhole at beg of row as follows: Rib 3, bind off 2 sts, work to end. On next row, cast on 2 sts over bound-off sts of last row. When ribbing measures 1½"/4.5cm, change to larger circular needles. Keeping first and last 7 sts in ribbing and working buttonhole as before every 2½ (2¾,2½)"/6 (6.5,6) cm, inc 1 st inside front band, continue in st st for 2 rows. Work color pattern following chart I. Continue in st st and ribbing band in MC until 12½ (13½,14)"/32 (34,35.5) cm from beg.

CHART I

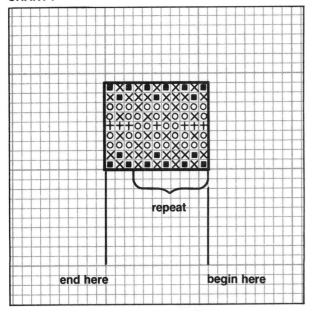

repeat

end here   begin here

KEY:

■ = MC (aubergine)

☒ = A (plum)

☐ = B (teal)

⊞ = C (magenta)

DIVIDE FOR BACK AND FRONT
Keeping to patterns, work 64 (68,72) sts and sl to holder for right front, k next 115 (123,131) sts for back; sl rem sts to holder for left front. Working back and forth on circular needle, bind off 6 (6,8) sts at beg of next 2 rows, then bind off 2 sts at beg of next 8 rows—87 (95,99) sts. Work even until 7½ (8½,9)"/19 (21.5,23) cm above dividing row.

SHAPE SHOULDERS
Bind off 8 (9,10) sts at beg of next 6 rows. Sl rem 39 (41,39) sts to holder for neckband.

FRONTS:
Sl sts for fronts to needle and, working both sides simultaneously, bind off at each armhole edge 6 (6,8) sts once and then 2 sts 4 times. Work even on 50 (54,56) sts until armhole measures 5 (6,6½)"/ 12.5 (15,16.5) cm. End with right side facing.

SHAPE NECK
Sl center 22 sts to holder, k to 22 sts from end; turn. Keeping to st st, dec 1 st at each neck edge every other row until 24 (27,30) sts rem. Work even until same length as back to shoulders; bind off from shoulder edge as for back.

SLEEVES
With smaller dp needles and MC, cast on 56 (56,60) sts. Join, taking care not to twist sts. Mark beg of row. Work 2½"/6cm in k 1, p 1 ribbing. Change to size 4 dp needles and work 1 rnd st st, inc 0 (0,4) sts evenly spaced around. Work pattern following chart II. Continue in st st, inc 1 st before and after marker every sixth rnd until there are 82 (88,94) sts. Work even until 15½ (16½,17½)"/39.5 (42,44.5) cm from beg.

CHART II

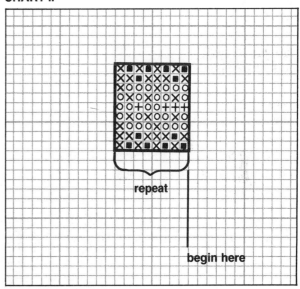

repeat

begin here

SHAPE CAP
Working back and forth, bind off 6 (6,8) sts at beg of next 2 rows, then 2 sts at beg of next 8 rows. Work even on 54 (60,62) sts until 5½ (6½,6⅔)"/14 (16.5,17) cm from beg. End with p row. K 2 tog across. Bind off all sts.

FINISHING

Sew shoulder seams. Neckband: With smaller dp needles and MC, work ribbing across sts from front band, place marker, k across sts on front holder, pick up and k 24 (29,29) sts to shoulder, k sts from back holder, pick up and k 24 (29,29) sts to front holder, k across sts on front holder, place marker, work in ribbing to end. Keeping sts at front edges in ribbing as established, p 1 rnd, inc 4 (0,2) sts evenly spaced between markers—112 (120,120) sts between markers. Work between markers in st st and pattern from chart III, and work 1 more buttonhole on front band on 5th row of chart. Work 1 more st st rnd in MC. Working in ribbing as established, continue ribbing between markers for 1 rnd. Bind off in ribbing. Block lightly, omitting ribbings. Sew in sleeves, easing to fit. Sew on buttons to correspond to buttonholes.

CHART III

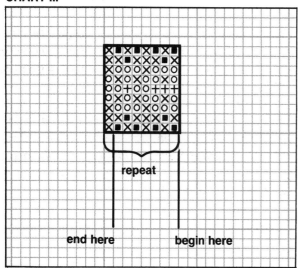

PULLOVER

SIZES

Directions are for girl's small, with medium and large in parentheses. Finished chest measurements 34½ (37,39⅓)"/87 (94,100) cm; length to back neck edge 19 (21,22½)"/48 (53.5,57) cm; armhole measures 12 (13,14)"/30.5 (33,35.5) cm; length of sleeve from underarm 15 (16,17)"/38 (40.5,43) cm.

MATERIALS

10 (12,14) oz/285 (340,400) cm Shetland wool in aubergine (MC), and 1oz/30gr each plum (A), teal (B), and magenta (C)

NEEDLES

One each size 2/2.75mm and size 4/3.5mm circular needles, or size needed to obtain gauge
One set size 4/3.5mm double-pointed knitting needles
Five size 2/2.75mm double-pointed needles
2 stitch holders

GAUGE

13 sts = 2"/5cm and 8 rows = 1"/2.5cm on size 4 needles over st st

BODY

With smaller circular needle and MC, cast on 224 (240,256) sts. Taking care not to twist sts, join, and work around in k 1, p 1 ribbing for 1½"/4cm. Mark beg of rnd; carry marker. Change to larger circular needle and work 2 rows st st (k every rnd). Work color pattern following chart. Continue in st st with MC until 12 (13,14)"/30.5 (33,35.5) cm from beg.

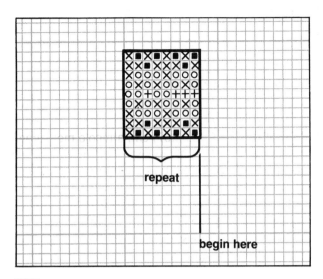

repeat

begin here

KEY:

■ = MC (aubergine)

⊠ = A (plum)

⊡ = B (teal)

⊞ = C (magenta)

DIVIDE FOR BACK AND FRONT

Keeping st st, work 112 (120,128) sts for front and sl to holder. Turn. Working back and forth on circular needle, bind off 6 (6,8) sts at beg of next 2 rows, then bind off 2 sts at beg of next 8 rows—84 (92,96) sts. Work even until 7 (8,8½)"/18 (20,21.5) cm above dividing row.

SHAPE SHOULDERS

Bind off 8 (9,10) sts at beg of next 6 rows. Sl rem 36 (38,36) sts to holder for neckband. Sl sts for front to needle and complete as for back until 5 (5½,6)"/13 (14,15) cm from dividing row. End with right side facing.

SHAPE NECK

Mark center 24 sts. Work to first marker; with 2nd strand, k to next marker and sl sts to holder for neck-band, work to end. Working both sides simulta-neously, dec 1 st at each neck edge every other row 6 (7,6) times. Work even until same length as back to shoulders. Bind off from each shoulder edge as for back.

SLEEVES

With smaller dp needles and MC, cast on 56 (56,60) sts, divided on 3 needles. Taking care not to twist sts, join, and work in k 1, p 1 ribbing for 2½"/6cm, inc 0 (0,4) sts evenly spaced on last rnd. Mark beg of rnd. Change to larger needles and st st, and work chart. Continue in st st with MC, inc 1 st before and after marker on every 6th rnd 11 (14,14) times—78 (84,92) sts. Work even until 15 (16,17)"/38 (40.5,43) cm from beg, ending 6 (6,8) sts before marker on last rnd.

SHAPE CAP

Bind off 12 (12,16) sts, dropping marker. Change to larger circular needle and, working back and forth, bind off 2 sts at beg of next 8 rows. Work even on 50 (56,60) sts until 5 (5¾,6)"/12.5 (14.5,15) cm from beg of cap shaping. End with right side facing. K 2 tog across. Bind off all sts.

FINISHING

Block lightly. Sew shoulder seams. Neckband: With 5 dp needles (using 4 needles for picked-up sts and 5th needle to work with) and MC, k across sts from back holder, pick up and k 24 (29,29) sts from front neck holder, k across 24 sts from front holder, pick up and k 24 (29,29) sts to shoulder. K 1 rnd, inc 4 (0,2) sts evenly spaced around—112 (120,120) sts. Work in pattern from chart. Work 1 rnd in MC, then 1 rnd in k 1, p 1 ribbing. Bind off in ribbing. Sew in sleeves, easing to fit. Block lightly.

COLORED COTTONS

WHAT COULD BE MORE COMFORTABLE THAN A COTTON SHORTS-AND-SWEATSHIRT
SET? I'VE USED A COMBINATION OF FRUITY COLORS, BUT YOU COULD
JUST AS EASILY USE ONE COLOR.

SWEATSHIRT

SIZES

Directions are for girl's small, with medium and large
in parentheses. Finished chest measurements 36
(38,41)"/91.5 (96.5,104) cm; armhole measures 16
(17¾,20)"/40.5 (45,51) cm; length of sleeve from
underarm 15 (16,17)"/38 (40.5,43) cm.

MATERIALS

14 (17½,21) oz/400 (500,600) gr worsted
weight cotton yarn in turquoise (MC),
2oz/60gr green (A), and 1oz/30gr each pink
(B) and orange (C)

NEEDLES

One pair each size 6/4mm and 8/5mm, or size
needed to obtain gauge
4 stitch holders
1 bobbin (optional)

GAUGE

4 sts and 5 rows = 1"/2.5cm on size 8 needles over
st st

BACK

With smaller needles and A, cast on 71 (75,81) sts.
Work in k 1, p 1 ribbing for 2"/5cm; inc 1 st at end of
last row. Change to larger needles, MC, and st st,
and work even until 14 (15,16)"/35.5 (38,40.5) cm
from beg. End with right side facing.

SHAPE ARMHOLES

Bind off 4 sts at beg of next 2 rows, then dec 1 st
each edge every other row until 28 sts rem. Sl sts to
holder for neckband.

FRONT

Note: When changing colors, be sure to pick up new
color under color just worked to avoid holes.

Work as for back until 50 sts rem. End with right side
facing.

PLACE PATTERN

Keeping to st st and continuing armhole dec, k 24 MC, k 2 A (using bobbin, if desired); with new strand of MC, work to end. Continue in st st, following chart beg row 2, until chart is completed. End with right side facing.

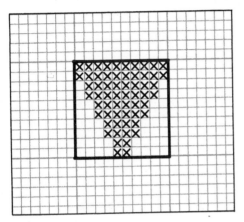

KEY:

☐ = MC (turquoise)

☒ = A (green)

SHAPE NECK

Mark center 24 sts. Continuing raglan dec, work to marker; with 2nd strand of yarn, k to next marker, sl sts between markers to holder, work to end. Working both sides simultaneously, dec 1 st each neck edge every other row 2 times. Work neck edge even while continuing raglan dec until 2 sts rem. K 2 tog. Fasten off.

SLEEVES

With smaller needles and B, cast on 35 (35,37) sts. Work in k 1, p 1 ribbing for 2"/5cm; inc 1 st at end of last row. Change to larger needles and MC, inc 1 st each edge every 4th row until there are 52 (56,62) sts. Work even until 15 (16,17)"/38 (40.5,43) cm from beg. End with right side facing.

SHAPE CAP

Bind off 4 sts at beg of next 2 rows, then dec 1 st each edge every other row until 8 sts rem. Sl sts to holder for neckband. Work 2nd sleeve in same manner, using C instead of B.

FINISHING

Block pieces lightly. Sew 3 of the raglan sleeve seams. Neckband: With smaller needles and A, k across 28 sts from back neck holder, 8 sts from left sleeve, pick up and k 13 sts to front neck holder, k across 24 sts from front neck holder, pick up and k 13 sts up right front neck edge, k 8 sts from right sleeve. Work in k 1, p 1 ribbing for 1"/2.5cm. Bind off loosely in ribbing. Weave remaining raglan, including neckband seam. Sew side and sleeve seams.

VEST

SIZES

Directions are for girl's small, with medium and large in parentheses. Finished chest measurements 37 (39,42)"/94 (99,106.5) cm; length to back neck edge 21 (23,25)"/53.5 (58.5,63.5) cm.

MATERIALS

10½ (10½,14) oz/300 (300,400) gr worsted weight cotton yarn in turquoise (MC), 3½oz/100gr green (A), and 1oz/30gr each pink (B) and orange (C) 7 gripper snaps

NEEDLES

One pair each size 6/4mm and 8/5mm needles, or size needed to obtain gauge 7 stitch holders

GAUGE

4 sts and 5 rows = 1"/2.5cm on size 5 needles over st st

BACK

Note: When changing colors, be sure to pick up new color under color just worked to avoid holes.

With smaller needles and A, cast on 74 (78,84) sts. Work in k 1, p 1 ribbing for 2"/5cm. Change to larger needles and MC, and continue in st st until 14 (15,16)"/35.5 (38,40.5) cm from beg. End with right side facing.

SHAPE ARMHOLES

Bind off 4 sts at beg of next 2 rows. Dec 1 st at each edge every other row 2 times. Work even in st st until armhole measures 7 (8,9)"/18 (20,23) cm. End with right side facing. Sl 20 (22,24) sts to holder for shoulder, 22 (22,24) sts to holder for neckband, and rem sts to holder for other shoulder.

RIGHT FRONT

With smaller needles and A, cast on 44 (46,50) sts. Work in k 1, p 1 ribbing for 2"/5cm. Change to larger needles and, keeping first 7 sts in ribbing in A, work even in st st on rem sts until 14 (15,16)"/35.5 (38,40.5) cm from beg. End with wrong side facing.

SHAPE ARMHOLE

Bind off 4 sts at beg of next row, then dec 1 st at armhole edge every other row twice. Work even until armhole measures 4 (5,6)"/10 (13,15) cm. End with right side facing.

SHAPE NECK

Work 14 (14,16) sts and sl to holder for neckband. Continue in st st, dec 1 st at neck edge every other row 4 times. Work even until same length as back to shoulder. Sl sts to holder.

LEFT FRONT

Work to correspond to right front, reversing shaping.

FINISHING

Join shoulders. Neckband: Right side facing, with smaller needles and A, work in k 1, p 1 ribbing across sts from right front holder, pick up and k 22 sts to shoulder, k across back neck holder. Pick up and k 22 sts to front neck holder, work ribbing across sts from front neck holder. Working in k 1, p 1 ribbing as established, dec 1 st at each end of row for 7 rows. Continue in ribbing until neckband measures 2¼"/5.75 cm. Bind off in ribbing. Fold neckband in half to wrong side and tack in place.

RIGHT ARMHOLE EDGING

Right side facing, with smaller needles and B, pick up and k 83 (91,99) sts around armhole edging. Work in k 1, p 1 ribbing for 1½"/3cm. Bind off all sts in ribbing.

LEFT ARMHOLE EDGING

With C, work as for right armhole. Sew side seams. Place gripper snaps evenly spaced along front bands.

SHORTS

SIZES

Directions are for girl's small, with medium and large in parentheses. Finished waist measurements (before elastic) 36 (38,41)"/91.5 (96.5,104) cm; length from hem to waist 13½ (15,16½)"/34 (38,41) cm.

MATERIALS

10½ (10½,14) oz/300 (300,400) gr worsted weight cotton yarn
¾"/3cm width elastic to fit waist

NEEDLES

One pair size 8/5mm needles, or size needed to obtain gauge

GAUGE

4 sts and 5 rows = 1"/2.5cm on size 8 needles over st st

(MAKE 2):

Cast on 92 (96,104) sts and work in st st for 1"/2.5cm, ending with p row. P 1 row for turning ridge. Continue in st st until 3½ (4,4½)"/8 (10,11) cm above turning ridge. End with right side facing.

SHAPE CROTCH

Bind off 6 sts at beg of next 2 rows, then dec 1 st each edge every other row 4 (4,5) times—72 (76,82) sts. Work even until 10 (11,12)"/25.5 (28,30.5)cm above beg of crotch shaping. End with p row. P 1 row on right side for turning ridge. Continue in st st for 1"/2.5cm. Bind off all sts.

FINISHING

Sew front and back seams from crotch to waist. Sew leg seams. Turn bottom hems to wrong side and sew in place. Turn top hem to wrong side and sew in place, leaving opening to insert elastic. Thread elastic through and adjust to fit; sew ends tog securely. Close opening.

COTTON GUERNSEY

A VARIATION ON A CLASSIC FISHERMAN'S SWEATER. HEAVY COTTON
YARN MAKES IT SUITABLE FOR YEAR-ROUND WEAR.

SIZES

Directions are for girl's or boy's small, with medium
and large in parentheses. Finished chest measurements 37 (40,43)"/94 (101,109) cm; length to back
neck edge 21 (23,25)"/54 (58.5,63.5) cm; armhole
measures 17 (19,21)"/43 (48,53.5) cm; length of
sleeve from underarm 17½ (18½,19½)"/43
(45.5,48) cm.

MATERIALS

28 (31½,31½) oz/800 (900,900) cm heavyweight
cotton yarn

NEEDLES

One 32"/81cm circular needle size 9/5.50mm, or
size needed to obtain gauge
One set each size 7/4.5mm and size 9/5.5mm
double-pointed needles
6 stitch holders
One 16"/40.5cm circular
needle size 9/5.50mm
(optional)

GAUGE

4 sts = 1"/2.5cm and 11 rnds =
2"/5cm on size 9 needles over st st

BODY

With 32" circular needle and MC, cast on 148
(160,172) sts. Taking care not to twist sts, join. Mark
beg of rnd; carry marker. Work *2 rnds p, 2 rnds k;
repeat from * 2 times. Continue in st st and work
even until 11 (12,13)"/28 (30.5,35.5) cm from beg.
Work pattern as follows:
Rnd 1: †P 12 (14,16), place marker; p 1, k 6, p 1,
place marker; *k 1, p 1; repeat from * 17 (18,19)
times, place marker; p 1, k 6, p 1, place marker; k 12
(14,16), place marker; repeat from † once. Carry
markers.

Rnd 2: †P 12 (14,16); p 1, k 6, p 1; *p 1, k 1; repeat
from * 17 (18,19) times; p 1, k 6, p 1; p 12 (14,16);
repeat from † once.
Rnd 3: †K 12 (14,16); p 1, k 6, p 1; *k 1, p 1; repeat
from * 17 (18,19) times; p 1, k 6, p 1; k 12 (14,16);
repeat from † once.
Rnd 4: †K 12 (14,16); p 1, k 6, p 1; *p 1, k 1; repeat
from * 17 (18,19) times; p 1, k 6, p 1; k 12 (14,16);
repeat from † once.
Rnd 5: †P 12 (14,16); p 1, sl 3 sts to cable needle
and hold in front, k 3, k 3 from cable needle; p 1; *k
1, p 1; repeat from * 17 (18,19) times; p 1, sl 3 sts to
cable needle and hold in front, k 3, k 3 from cable
needle, p 1; p 12 (14,16); repeat from † once.

Rnds 6 through 8: Repeat rnds 2 through 4.
Repeat these 8 rnds for pattern until 13 (14,15)"/33
(35.5,38) cm from beg.

DIVIDE FOR FRONT AND BACK:

Work across 74 (80,84) sts for back. Sl rem sts to holder for front. Keeping to patterns as established, working back and forth on circular needles, bind off 2 sts at beg of next 2 rows. Work even until 8 (9,10)"/20 (23,25.5) cm from dividing row. Sl 22 (25,28) sts to holder for shoulder, 26 sts to holder for neckband, and rem sts to holder for other shoulder. Sl sts for front to circular needle and work as for back until 5 (6,7)"/13 (15,18) cm from dividing row. End with right side facing.

SHAPE NECK

Mark center 20 sts. Work in pattern to first marker; with new strand, work to next marker, sl sts between markers to holder for neckband, work to end. Working both sides simultaneously, dec 1 st at each neck edge every other row 3 times. Work even until same length as back to shoulders. Sl sts to holder.

SLEEVES

With smaller dp needles and MC, cast on 36 (36,40) sts. Taking care not to twist sts, join and work in twisted ribbing (k 1 in back of st, p 1) for 2½"/3cm. Mark beg of rnd; carry markers. Change to larger dp needles and st st, and inc as follows: *k 1, inc 1 in next st; repeat from * around—54 (54,60) sts. Continue in st st, inc 1 st on either side of marker on next rnd, then every 6th rnd, 6 (10,11) times more—68 (76,84) sts. Work even until 13½ (14½,15½)"/33 (35.5,38) cm from beg. P 2 rnds, k 2 rnds, p 2 rnds, inc 1 st on last rnd. Seed st rnd: *K 1, p 1; repeat from * around. Repeat seed st rnd until 2"/5cm of seed st are worked. P 2 rnds, k 2 rnds, p 2 rnds. Bind off.

FINISHING

Weave or sew shoulder seams. Neckband: With smaller dp needles or 16"/40.5cm circular needle, right side facing, k across sts from back neck holder, pick up and k 16 sts to front neck edge, k 20 sts from front neck holder, pick up and k 16 sts to shoulder. P 1 rnd. Work in twisted ribbing for 1"/2.5cm. Bind off in ribbing. Sew in sleeves, easing to fit. Steam seams lightly.

RIBBONED STOLE AND CLUTCH

**A VERY SPECIAL WRAP AND MATCHING PURSE FOR THE PROM.
CHOOSE A COLOR THAT MATCHES THE GOWN.**

STOLE

SIZE
One size fits all. Finished stole measures
16"/40.5cm by 70"/178cm, including fringe.

Materials
14oz/400gr worsted weight brushed acrylic,
12yds/11m each of ⅜"/1cm width single-faced satin
ribbon and ⅜"/1cm width textured flowered ribbon
Fabric defrayer

CROCHET HOOK
One size H/5mm crochet hook, or size needed to
obtain gauge

GAUGE
13 sc = 4"/10cm; 3 rows sc and 1 row dc =
1¼"/3cm with size H hook.

Ch 211 to measure about 65"/165cm.
Row 1: Sc in 2nd ch from hook and each rem ch.
Row 2: Ch 1, turn; sc in each st across.
Row 3: Rep row 2.
Row 4: Ch 3 (counts as first dc), turn; dc in each rem
sc.
Row 5: Rep row 2.
Rep rows 2 through 5 eleven times more. Rep row 2
twice more. Do not fasten off.

EDGING
Edging row: *Ch 3, sk 1 st, sl st in next st; repeat
from * across. Fasten off. Attach yarn to other
lengthwise edge at beg of starting ch with right side
facing. Working along other side of starting ch, work
as for edging row.

FINISHING
Cut ribbon to 70"/178cm lengths. Weave satin
through first dc row, under first dc, *over next, under
next; rep from * across. Weave flowered ribbon
through next dc row, over first dc, *under next, over
next; repeat from * across. Taking care to leave ex-
cess ribbon evenly divided at beg and end of row,
weave ribbon through every dc row, alternating
weaving pattern and alternating satin and flowered
ribbons. Treat ribbon ends with fabric defrayer for
greater wear and washability. Wrap yarn around a
3"/7.5cm piece of cardboard; cut for fringe. Using 2
strands of yarn and crochet hook, loop strands
through ends of sc rows on width of stole between
ribbons.

CLUTCH

SIZES

Clutch fabric measures 8½"/21.5cm by 15¾"/40cm. Finished measurements are 8½"/21.5cm by 5"/12.5cm.

MATERIALS

1¾oz/50gr worsted weight brushed acrylic
4yds/4m each ⅜"/1cm wide single-faced satin ribbon and textured flowered ribbon
¼yd/22cm lining fabric
7"/10cm matching zipper
Sewing needle and matching thread

CROCHET HOOK

One size H/5mm crochet hook, or size needed to obtain gauge

GAUGE

13 dc = 4"/10cm; 4 rows dc = 2¼"/6cm with size H hook

Ch 29. Row 1: Dc in 4th ch from hook and each rem ch. Row 2: Ch 3 (counts as 1 dc), turn; dc in each dc across. Rep row 2 until 26 rows from beg. Do not fasten off.

EDGING

†*Ch 3, sk 1 st, sl st in next st; rep from * across row; **ch 3, working along side of rows, sl st in next st; rep from ** to starting ch; working along opposite side of starting ch and up other edge, rep from † once. Fasten off.

FINISHING

Cut ribbon into 10"/25cm lengths. Weave satin through first row, under first dc, *over next, under next; rep from * across. Weave flowered ribbon through next row, over first dc, *under next, over next; rep from * across. Weave ribbon through every row, alternating weaving pattern and alternating satin and flowered ribbons. Cut lining fabric to rectangle 9"/23cm by 16"/40.5cm. Turn edges under to fit and iron. Whipstitch lining to clutch. Fold as desired. Sew side seams. Sew zipper in place to close.

Yarn Suppliers

Camouflage-and-Suede Pullover
EMU Superwash double knitting yarn from:

Plymouth Yarn Co.
P. O. Box 28
Bristol, PA 19007

Peplumed Diamonds
Windmist from:

Brunswick Yarns
P. O. Box 276
Pickens, SC 29671

Glittery Diamonds
same as above

Arrow Raglan
Red Heart 4-Ply Knit & Crochet Yarn from:

Coats & Clark
P. O. Box 1010
Toccoa, GA 30577

Pencil-Striped Pullover
2-Ply Homespun and Fisherman yarns from:

Bartlettyarns
Harmony, ME 04942

Summer Mesh Top
Patons Cotton Perle from:

Susan Bates/Patons
Route 9A
Chester, CT 06412

Fishnet Vest and Scarf
Jewel from:

William Unger & Company, Inc.
230 Fifth Avenue
New York, NY 10001

Vertical-Striped V-neck
Pomfret 100% Wool Sport Yarn from:

Brunswick Yarns
P. O. Box 276
Pickens, SC 29671

Staid Plaid
Softball 100% Pure Wool Yarn from:

Conshohocken Cotton Company
Ford Bridge Road
Conshohocken, PA 19428

Mad Plaid
same as above

Crayon Horizontal Vest
Fore-'n-Aft Acrylic Sport Yarn from:

Brunswick Yarns
P. O. Box 276
Pickens, SC 29671

Sporty Stripes
same as above

Fair Isle Vest and Matching Tie
Shetland Style Fine 2-Ply Yarns from:

Harrisville Designs
Harrisville, NH 03450

Jungle Print
Pronostic from:

Phildar, Inc.
Fashion Knitting Yarns
6438 Dawson Blvd.
Norcross, GA 30093

French Sailor Shirt
Cassino from:

Bernat Yarn & Craft Corporation
Uxbridge, MA 01569

Snowflake Ragg Pullover and Ski Hat
Green Mountain Spinnery 100% Wool Yarn from:

Green Mountain Spinnery
P. O. Box 54
Putney, VT 05346

Boucle Pullover Jacket and Cloche
Mardi Gras and Landscape Chunky from:

Plymouth Yarn Company
P. O. Box 28
Bristol, PA 19007

Silk Blend Tunics
Chelsea Silk and Saratoga from:

Tahki Imports Ltd.
92 Kennedy Street
Hackensack, NJ 07601

Ballerina Vest and Legwarmers
Patons Solo DK from:

Susan Bates/Patons
Route 9A
Chester, CT 06412

Ribbon from:

C. M. Offray and Son, Inc.
Chester, NJ 07930

Icelandic Pullover
Icelandic Kurlie Lamb and Lopi Light from:

Reynolds Yarns Inc.
15 Oser Avenue
Hauppauge, NY 11788

Girl's Icelandic Outerwear—Vest, Socks, Hat, and
Mittens
4-Ply Soft Wool Clothing Yarn and Pebbles from:

Wilde Yarns
3705 Main Street
Philadelphia, PA 19127

Boy's Icelandic Vest and Hat
same as above

Feminine Fair Isle Sweater Set
Shetland Style Fine 2-Ply Yarns from:

Harrisville Designs
Harrisville, NH 03450

Colored Cottons
Softball 100% Combed Cotton Yarn from:

Conshohocken Cotton Company
Ford Bridge Road
Conshohocken, PA 19428

Cotton Guernsey
Gloucester from:

Bernat Yarn & Craft Corporation
Uxbridge, MA 01569

Ribboned Stole and Clutch
Windmist from:

Brunswick Yarns
P. O. Box 276
Pickens, SC 29671

Ribbon from:

C. M. Offray and Son, Inc.
Chester, NJ 07930

ABOUT THE AUTHOR

Michele Maks started knitting when she was ten years old, and in the past decade she's created several hundred pieces for children and teens. In 1985 she started selling her designs to magazines such as *Woman's World*, *Better Homes & Gardens*, *McCall's Needlework & Crafts*, *Knitting with Simplicity*, and *Herrschner's Crochet*. She also creates one-of-a-kind garments for specialty shops and private clients, as well as mail-order ready-to-wear machine knits for children. A native of Long Island, New York, Ms. Maks now lives on a beautiful 165-acre farm in Maine with her husband, Jack Carson, and children, Quayl, Tobin, Tesseract, and Tobias.